THE TOP 100 RECIPES for HAPPY KIDS

THE TOP 100 RECIPES for HAPPY KIDS

KEEP YOUR CHILD ALERT, FOCUSED, ACTIVE, AND HEALTHY

Charlotte Watts Dip.ION and Gemini Adams

DUNCAN BAIRD PUBLISHERS
LONDON

The Top 100 Recipes for Happy Kids
Charlotte Watts and Gemini Adams

Distributed in the USA and Canada by
Sterling Publishing Co., Inc.
387 Park Avenue South
New York, NY 10016-8810

This edition first published in the UK and USA in 2007 by
Duncan Baird Publishers Ltd
Sixth Floor, Castle House
75–76 Wells Street
London W1T 3QH

Managing Editor: Grace Cheetham
Editors: Emma Callery and Judy Barratt
Managing Designer: Daniel Sturges
Commissioned photography: William Lingwood
Food stylist: Joss Herd
Prop stylist: Helen Trent

Library of Congress Cataloging-in-Publication Data
Available

ISBN: 978-1-84483-603-1

10 9 8 7 6 5 4 3

Dedicated to the future generation. We share this knowledge so that they may gain an understanding of the integral relationship between food, nature, and nurture, and receive the many benefits to mind, body, and soul.

Typeset in Helvetica Condensed
Color reproduction by Colourscan, Singapore
Printed in China by Imago

For information about custom editions, special sales,
premium and corporate purchases, please contact
Sterling Special Sales Department at 800-805-5489 or
specialsales@sterlingpub.com.

Publisher's Note
This book is not intended as a replacement for professional medical advice and treatment. The publishers and authors cannot accept any responsibility for any illness or damage incurred as a result of using any of the therapeutic methods or advice contained in this work. If you or your child suffers from any medical condition that makes you unsure as to the suitability of any of the advice or recipes in this book, consult your medical practitioner before using them.

Measurements
1 tsp = 5ml
1 tbsp = 15ml
1 cup = 225ml

contents

KEY TO SYMBOLS

Suitable for vegetarians: Recipes showing this symbol contain no animal products. Vegetarian recipes can be a good choice for children suffering from digestive problems or from inflammatory conditions, such as eczema, asthma, and acne.

Wheat free: Wheat is used in foods as a bulking agent, but it can be difficult to digest. Replace it with corn, buckwheat, rice, tapioca, and rye flours. You can find wheat-free breads, tortillas and tart and pizza crusts in health-food stores.

Gluten free: Gluten is the substance in wheat, rye, barley, and oats that adds "stickiness" to bread and other baked goods. Gluten intolerance in children can cause inflammation, depression, and digestive problems. Gluten-free grains include buckwheat, millet, and corn.

Dairy free: Cow's milk can be the cause of nasal blockages and sinusitis, catarrh, and throat and chest infections. It can also trigger conditions such as asthma, eczema, and acne. Try rice, almond, or oat milk, or soymilk and unsweetened soy yogurt as alternatives.

Contains eggs: If your child has an egg intolerance, it is even more important to give them fresh foods, as egg is often used commercially as a binding agent and thickener. Substitutes for baking are made from arrowroot and agar-agar.

Contains nuts: Many children have a nut allergy, so we have avoided nuts in many dishes. However, you can replace nuts with seeds, such as pumpkin seeds, that you know your child can eat. Never give whole nuts to children aged under five years as they can cause choking.

INTRODUCTION

Your child's happiness is of the utmost importance. Increasingly, we are recognizing that diet plays a crucial part in achieving that happiness, because it has a fundamental impact on the health of the body—and by extension the mind and emotions. It stands to reason, then, that one of the best ways to help your child be happy is to choose and cook good-quality, nutritious food.

In recent years the nutritional and scientific communities have conducted a great deal of research into the links between food and its effects on children's health and well-being. It is well known that maintaining balanced blood-sugar levels helps to maintain stable moods, and encouraging a healthy digestive system can relieve many upsetting conditions, such as wind and bloating. Likewise, it is clearly documented that a lack of essential nutrients can reduce a child's immune function. A poorly nourished child is more likely to become ill, and less able to participate in school life and socializing with friends—crucial factors for their development and overall happiness.

Feeling successful and being praised for achievement, whether in general development for smaller children, or academic success for older children, have a huge impact on a child's confidence and self-esteem—literally, on their happiness with themselves. New evidence clearly links a child's nutritional intake with his or her academic performance. The American School Food Service Association found that 4th-grade students (aged 8 to 9 years) who received the least amount of protein in their diets had the lowest achievement scores. In addition, studies show that increasing dietary sources of B vitamins, vitamin C, and the minerals zinc, iron, and magnesium positively affect a child's brain function and development.

In this book we present foods and recipes that aim to optimize the happiness of children aged between 4 and 12 years. An overhaul of your child's diet might at first seem challenging, especially if you are used to buying convenience foods, but we have created the book's 100 recipes with simplicity and speed in mind, to make the transition to a healthy diet for the whole family both painless and fun.

FOOD LABELING

Food manufacturers are obliged to list all ingredients in their foods. The more conscientious will state any commonly intolerant ingredients. Many stores and health-food stores have specific sections for "gluten-free" and "dairy-free." Ask staff for help, and read labels to get used to identifying brands and products that tend to include ingredients your child cannot tolerate.

Recognizing the right foods

To improve your child's happiness through diet, we advocate using natural, whole foods, comprising fresh produce as much as possible. In each recipe we explain how the ingredients directly contribute to your child's nutritional needs and suggest ways to combine foods, for balance and variety. Each recipe also has a series of symbols to guide you with any special dietary needs (see key, page 6).

Unless otherwise stated:

- Use large eggs
- Use fresh herbs
- Wash all fruit and vegetables before preparing them
- Choose organic, especially meat and dairy, to expose your child to fewer hormones and antibiotics

GOOD NUTRITION = HAPPIER KIDS

It really is easy to achieve the basics of optimum nutrition by using ingredients that are whole foods—in other words, those that by and large do not come from a package, but are natural, fresh, and preferably organic. Avoid processed foods, which often have added preservatives and colors, many of which can be harmful to developing bodies. Of course, it is challenging to avoid such products altogether, so we recommend an 80:20 ratio, whereby you aim to use 80 percent whole foods in your child's diet, allowing 20 percent for occasional convenience foods. By following this advice, you will begin to:

- balance blood sugar
- encourage development
- improve digestion, and
- strengthen immunity

Balancing blood sugar

Achieving a good blood-sugar balance is crucial to your child's happiness. Sugar provides the energy your child needs to power everything that happens in his or her body, including energy levels, concentration, and how your child feels. To optimize their body processes, your child needs a regulated, steady supply of sugar from the right sources. We break down sugars (to glucose) from the carbohydrates (plant foods) we eat. The best sources of these sugars are fruit, vegetables, whole grains, nuts, seeds, and legumes. Although many processed foods children eat are very sweet, the sugar enters the bloodstream too quickly. These "empty" calories cause a surge of energy with little nutritional value. The worst culprits include candies, cakes, chocolate, snack bars, processed cereals (including white bread), and sodas and other sugary drinks. Because these foods require little breaking down in the body, they don't give your child a sustainable release of energy.

But what does this mean for happiness? Well, sweet, processed foods lead to sudden surges in energy, which are followed inevitably by energy dips and mood swings. A child with fluctuating blood-sugar levels can suffer from irritability, hyperactivity, energy slumps, headaches, poor concentration, and dizziness. Many experts believe that the increasing incidents of obesity and conditions such as attention deficit and hyperactivity disorder (ADHD) in children have their roots in blood-sugar imbalance.

By achieving a good blood-sugar balance for your child, you can bring about great improvements in their mood, sleep, digestion, stress response, skin health, and weight management.

One of the best ways to stabilize blood sugar is to provide a healthy, balanced start to the day. Make breakfast a priority—a proper mealtime rather than a rushed snack wolfed down while racing against the clock. When your child wakes up, he or she has been without food for many hours and needs sustenance to bring his or her blood-sugar level gently back up and to provide fuel and nutrients for the day ahead. Studies have shown that children who eat breakfast and a healthy midmorning snack are less likely to fill up later on saturated fat and "empty" calories. Protein (from such foods as eggs, nuts, seeds, yogurt, and whole grains) is especially important at breakfast, as it helps to create all the chemicals the body needs to function throughout the day and slows down the release of sugars.

Here are some more pointers to help you stabilize your child's blood-sugar balance for the rest of the day:

- Whenever possible at lunch and dinner, give your child plenty of vegetables, fruits, beans and lgumes, seeds, nuts, and whole grains, such as oats, whole wheat, brown rice, rye, and millet.
- Change refined "white" sources of bread, rice, and pasta to wholegrain or "brown" versions, which have their fiber left intact. This slows down the release of sugar into the bloodstream.
- Don't give candies, chocolate, cakes, cookies, and pastries as snacks—save them for rare treats. Instead, try fruit, savory snacks, and healthy nut-and-seed and granola bars, which cause fewer energy highs and lows.
- Reduce sugary drinks and sodas. Don't be fooled by clever marketing—check labels for sugar content and, when possible, offer diluted fruit juices, natural smoothies or, preferably, water.
- Keep desserts free from added sugar and give your child slow sugar-release fruits—peaches, blackberries, blueberries, raspberries, plums, strawberries, apricots (fresh and dried), figs, apples, pineapple (fresh), cherries, oranges, melon, and watermelon.

Encouraging brain development

Children's brains demand a steady supply of nutrients, particularly in the first 16 years of life, when the brain is growing at a continually high rate. As well as the American School Food Service Association study (see page 8), numerous other studies show the beneficial link between nutrition and children's mental development. In one, giving a daily multivitamin and mineral supplement to US schoolchildren aged 6 to 12 years led to marked increases in IQ scores and academic performance. Studies also show that children with anemia (low levels of iron in their blood) achieve lower scores in school tests than nonanemic children, indicating that iron is one of the most important nutrients for optimum brain development. So, to encourage healthy mental development in your child:

- Give him or her a child-friendly multivitamin and mineral supplement.
- Boost your child's intake of iron-rich foods, such as green leafy vegetables, whole grains, and red meat.
- Make sure he or she eats a good mix of dietary protein, including fish, chicken, turkey, bananas, yogurt, eggs, beans, nuts (especially almonds), seeds, quinoa, cottage cheese, avocados, and wholegrain crackers.
- Give him or her oily fish two or three times a week—the essential fatty acids, known as omega-3 oils, that they contain are crucial for your child's brain development and function.

Improving digestion

Encouraging a healthy digestive system is the next important step to raising a happy child. As with anything that is growing and developing, a child's digestive tract needs nurturing, otherwise it is prone to problems. Choosing foods that do not irritate the stomach and intestines and that contain nutrients the stomach can absorb easily can greatly reduce the incidence of annoying tummy upsets among children.

Healthy digestion is also crucial for the full and safe removal of toxins from the body; any build-up of these toxins in the gut can lead to digestive problems and allow toxins to circulate around the body, adding to the load on the immune system. Digestive disorders, such as constipation, diarrhea, wind, bloating, and stomach pain, can all be a direct effect of toxicity. These symptoms are common in children who eat too many processed foods, which are often high in additives.

Processed foods also tend to be high in nonbeneficial sugars, which feed harmful bacteria in the gut. These unwelcome guests then crowd out the beneficial bacteria that should make up about 80 percent of the gut's bacteria. These good bacteria, or probiotics, are crucial for many aspects of health, acting as our first line of immune defense. They are killed off not only by sugar, but also by antibiotics, stimulants, and stress. Low levels of beneficial bacteria are common in children with eczema, acne, ADHD, autism, psoriasis, and ear, nose, and throat problems, as well as digestive upsets. To help feed and promote beneficial bacteria and overall gut health, consider the following for your child:

- Increase his or her fiber intake. A whole-food diet of fruit and vegetables, nuts, grains, legumes, and seeds helps to provide a good level of fiber.
- Give them yogurt containing live cultures often.
- Cook them meals containing oily fish, such as mackerel and salmon, two or three times a week. The omega-3 oils are important for gut health.
- Make sure your child drinks 2½ to 7¾ cups of fluids a day in the form of

A QUICK GUIDE TO ANTIOXIDANTS

This table lists the main antioxidants, and their other healthy actions and main food sources.

Antioxidant	Actions	Food sources
Bioflavonoids	• Natural, antioxidant plant chemicals that also help other antioxidant nutrients, such as vitamin C, to work; increase circulation	• Greens, yellows, reds, oranges, purples, and blues! Particularly berries, broccoli, garlic, ginger, pineapples, red bell peppers
Selenium	• Helps the body to manufacture more of its own antioxidant enzymes; also boosts immunity by helping to produce antibodies	• Nuts and seeds, especially Brazil nuts (the amount depends upon the selenium content of the soil, so organic is best)
Vitamin A (animal) beta-carotene (plant)	• Fat-soluble, so these antioxidants travel with fats and work in fatty areas of the body, such as the eyes, heart, skin, and liver; very important for healing of the skin and gut	• Animal sources: dairy produce, eggs, fish oils, liver • Vegetable sources: dark green leafy vegetables, orange/yellow fruits and vegetables
Vitamin C	• Shown to have a preventative effect against many diseases; it helps the immune system to fight off infection and supports the liver in eliminating toxins associated with disease	• Apples, black currants, broccoli, Brussels sprouts, cauliflowers, citrus fruits, kiwis, papaya, red and green bell peppers, strawberries, tomatoes, watercress
Vitamin E	• Fat-soluble, so antioxidant action prevents damage to fatty areas, such as the brain, liver, kidneys and heart; important for hormone development	• Avocados, green leafy vegetables, nuts, oily fish (such as salmon, herring, tuna, sardines, mackerel), olives, whole grains, vegetable oils
Zinc	• A vital antioxidant for most immune processes, as well as for healing and growth	• Leafy and root vegetables, meat, nuts, seeds, peanuts, egg yolks, whole grains, beans

water, fruit teas (which can be cooled down), and diluted fruit juice. Good stool formation and the production of gastric and digestive juices rely on drinking plenty of water.

- Encourage regular exercise. This is essential for all body systems, but digestion in particular relies upon good muscle tone for optimum function.

Strengthening immunity

A child's body is constantly bombarded by new bacteria and viruses. This onslaught is a vital part of "priming" the immune system, and helps to develop a child's "immune memory," so the immune system can fight off the same invaders the next time they try to attack. Strengthening your child's immune system can improve his or her happiness through wellness, and help the body cope with many environmental toxins, including pollution and food additives.

One of the most important ways to help your child's immune system is to optimize their intake of antioxidants. These natural chemicals neutralize free radicals, harmful substances that damage cells and tissues, causing disease, and generally impair immune and other body functions. Constant exposure to free radicals from sunlight, pollutants, air travel, fried foods, and emissions from TVs, computers, and other appliances, means your child's need for antioxidants is greater than ever before.

The most important antioxidants, and their other actions on the body, are given in the table opposite. Include them in your child's diet as often as you can. The tables on the following pages provide a general guide to the macro- and micronutrients in foods that promote all aspects of your child's health.

A QUICK GUIDE TO MACRONUTRIENTS

Macronutrients are important for energy and most provide nutritional building blocks.

Nutrient	Actions	Food sources	How often?
Proteins	• Made of amino acids that aid growth and renewal of bones, teeth and skin • Produce antibodies for immune function • Produce many hormones	• Eggs, skinless turkey/chicken breast, fish • In plant foods, such as nuts, seeds, legumes, vegetables	• A small amount with every meal
Carbo-hydrates	• Our bodies break down carbohydrates to form glucose for energy • Carbohydrates are our main food source	• Vegetables, fruit, beans, legumes, nuts, seeds, and grains in their most whole, unprocessed forms	• 3 to 4 portions fruits or vegetables/day; 1 portion per meal of grains, seeds, etc
Essential fatty acids (EFAs) and monounsaturated fats	• EFAs: vital for hormone development, digestion, skin, immunity • Monounsaturated fats: prevent disease, protect body tissues	• EFAs: Omega 3s: oily fish; omega 6s: nuts, veg • Mono-unsaturated fats: olives, avocados, nuts	• Omega 3s: 2 to 3 times/week • Omega 6: daily • Monounsaturated fats: few times/week
Saturated fats	• Eating too many can result in digestion and circulation problems, but they are vital for cell communication, helping your child to move and think	• Animal sources, meat and dairy produce (choose organic to avoid toxins)	• Several times/week
BAD FATS Trans fats and hydrogenated fats	• Trans fats are damaged by cooking so can damage the body • Hydrogenated fats are processed in factories so can damage the cellular structure	• Junk food, especially potato chips, french fries, fried snacks	• Avoid as much as possible

A QUICK GUIDE TO MICRONUTRIENTS

Micronutrients, carried into the body by macronutrients, support essential body processes.

Nutrient	Actions	Food sources	How often?
Vitamins A, D and E (fat-soluble vitamins)	• Vitamins A and E promote growth and healing of all body tissues • Vitamin D promotes healthy bones and stable moods	• A and E: foods with oils and fats, whole grains • D: butter, meat, fish (mainly sunlight)	• Daily
B vitamins	• B vitamins allow us to unlock the energy from the food we eat; they are necessary for digestion, skin health, and all mental processes	• Whole foods, such as brown rice, whole grains, vegetables, beans, legumes, nuts, seeds, fish	• Daily portion of at least 3 of these foods
Vitamin C	• Supports skin and digestive health and prevents illness, such as frequent infections, constipation, bleeding gums, and asthma	• All the fruit and vegetables that your child will eat!	• Daily
Minerals (calcium, iron, magnesium, zinc, in particular)	• Responsible for electrical activity in the brain and nervous system and formation of bones and teeth • Calcium and magnesium calm the nervous system, adding to feelings of well-being; they are also crucial for brain function, growth and the digestive process • Iron is necessary for energy production • Zinc is used in large amounts for growth and development	• Calcium: fish, leafy vegetables, milk, nuts, whole grains • Iron: green leafy vegetables, red meat • Magnesium: fish, green leafy veg, nuts, whole grains • Zinc: fish, nuts and seeds	• Daily for each mineral

MOOD FOODS

While improving your child's digestion and blood-sugar balance will influence their happiness by improving overall health and well-being, offering foods that specifically influence mood will have a direct impact on how positive and confident your child feels. Certain foods, often known as "mood foods," contain amino acids the body can convert to the neurotransmitters dopamine and serotonin—the "happy chemicals" that make us feel good—as well as providing the vitamins and minerals the body needs for this conversion to take place.

The two most important amino acids that affect mood are tyrosine, which the body uses to make dopamine, and tryptophan, which it uses to produce serotonin. Increased levels of dopamine will raise your child's mood and keep them alert and energized throughout the day. Tyrosine-rich foods include lean meat, and dairy, fish, eggs, seafood, and lentils. Papaya contains high levels of the protein-digesting enzyme papain, which promotes good digestive health with the added bonus that papain itself contains high levels of tyrosine, making it the perfect lunch-box fruit snack. The feel-good chemical serotonin is often known for its natural pain-killing and sleep-regulating qualities. It promotes a relaxed happiness, ideal toward the end of the day. Provide early suppers that contain tryptophan-rich foods, such as cottage cheese, lamb, tuna, and poultry (see also box, opposite). To allow the passage of tryptophan into the brain, and to maximize the production of serotonin, complement these foods with others rich in complex carbohydrates, such as brown basmati rice or a small baked potato.

THE TOP MOOD FOODS

Food	Active ingredients	How often?
Asparagus, peas, spinach	• Mood-enhancing nutrients such as B vitamins, magnesium and calcium	• One or more every few days
Black beans, sunflower seeds, watercress	• Phenylalanine, which helps to increase the production of "happy" endorphins	• As often as possible
Cottage cheese, fish, lamb, lentils, peanuts, and pumpkin and sesame seeds	• Tryptophan, which the body uses to make serotonin, and protein for blood-sugar balance	• As often as possible
Green leafy vegetables: cabbage, watercress, spinach, arugula, kale	• Calcium and magnesium, which calm the nervous system and the gut	• Daily
Molasses	• Trace materials that are important for brain function	• Weekly (use instead of refined white sugar)
Nuts, seeds and their oils, or a good-quality supplement of these	• Fat-soluble antioxidants to protect the brain against action of free radicals; almonds combat sugar cravings; walnuts contain an antidepressant factor	• Daily (raw, unsalted varieties only)
Oily fish, such as salmon, trout, sardines, anchovies, pilchards	• A compound called uridine that reduces symptoms of depression • Omega-3 oils, needed for brain function	• 2 to 3 times a week

FOOD IS FUN

The whole family can eat and enjoy the recipes in this book and we urge you to make them for everyone, adults and children alike. Sitting down for meals as a family is a vital part of a child's relationship with food. Even if there are just two of you, eating the same foods at the table together can encourage an open-minded attitude to food. This will give your child an appreciation of healthy foods that hopefully will last them a lifetime, and will undoubtedly encourage them to experiment with foods that they have never seen before or have previously been unwilling to try.

To make mealtimes fun:

- Introduce games about food—who can guess where in the world a food comes from, how it's grown, and so on.
- Encourage your child to grow his or her own food, even if it is just a pot of herbs on a windowsill. This helps to improve a child's understanding of the relationship between nature, nurture, and food. A child is more likely to enjoy what they are eating if they have grown and cared for it themselves, giving them a great sense of achievement.
- Encourage your child to join you in the kitchen. Ask them to help you prepare foods; open their appreciation of flavors and seasoning by inviting them to enjoy and participate in all stages of the cooking process.

Introducing new foods

A child's development goes through many stages, and that applies to learning to appreciate new foods and being ready for new experiences as much as it does to walking and talking. Here are some ideas to make introducing new foods easier:

- Give unfamiliar foods in small amounts

on the side of the plate with little fuss and no insistence that your child eats them. Even if your child leaves them the first few times, after seeing them for the fifth time, he or she might just make that decision to try.

- Mix new foods with old favorites: try adding a new vegetable to a pizza or in a soup or stir-fry; or simply hide new foods in wraps, mashed in with others, and in stews.
- Eat the food yourself in front of your child for several days before offering it to him or her—you might find that your child even asks to try it.

Making shopping fun

As well as the growing and preparation of food, shopping and helping to make decisions about what you will all eat can help to increase children's interest in and awareness of food. To make trips to the supermarket a pleasant experience:

- Make sure no one is hungry—your choices can be hasty, tempers can be fraught, and "quick-fix" foods often seem more appealing.
- Learn the layout of your store or supermarket and avoid "problem areas," such as the cookie aisle.
- Invite your children to explore the foods they see in the store—allow each child to choose one healthy item to buy that they haven't tried before.

Ultimately, if your child's diet is "good" 80 percent of the time, then their body should be able to handle 20 percent "bad." This means you don't have to deny your children the odd sugary treat or bag of chips, so no one should feel deprived of anything, but the result is a happier, healthier family all round!

BREAKFASTS

Breakfast really is the most important meal of the day. It is well documented that kids who start the day "feasting like a king" will be happier right up until bedtime. If, during the day, a child's blood-sugar levels are stable, their mood, energy levels, and general well-being will be, too. All of the breakfast recipes contain good sources of fibre and protein to moderate blood-sugar levels, and stave off hunger pangs and the resulting energy dips. Whether you choose an on-the-go meal, such as blueberry and apple muffins, or a more substantial all-in-one meal, such as asparagus egg scramble, these delicious recipes will guarantee a happier and healthier start to the day.

rejuvenating juice

This is a great alternative to cartons of juice, which have added sugar and are often made from concentrates, removing goodness. This juice has extremely high doses of vitamins C and A, which your child needs for immunity, and of potassium for nerve function.

SERVES 2

PREPARATION
10 minutes

STORAGE
Refrigerate up to 1 day, then stir and serve.

TRY THIS WITH...
a teaspoon of grated root ginger for an extra bite—it will also help ward off colds.

HIGH IN...
potassium and vitamins A and C.

PROPERTIES
Celery is high in the mineral potassium, which helps to balance fluids in the body, reducing bloating and protecting your child's heart.

4 carrots
1 lemon
4 oranges
3 apples
6 celery sticks
2 celery tops

1 Peel the carrots, lemon, and oranges. Squeeze the juice from the lemon.

2 Cut the apples in half, then remove the cores, but leave the skins on.

3 Put all the fruit and celery sticks through a juicer, collecting the juice in a pitcher. Add the lemon juice to the fruit and celery mixture and stir well. Serve in glasses with straws. Garnish with the celery tops.

almond butter bites

Almonds are a true "superfood"—they are a nutritional powerhouse packed full of micronutrients, such as omega-6 oils and zinc. This alternative to peanut butter is simple to make and, as well as at breakfast, is delicious as an afternoon snack or a dessert topping.

11/4 cups toasted whole almonds
2 tablespoons olive oil
scant 1/2 cup chopped toasted almonds
2 slices wholegrain or sunflower bread

1 Place the whole almonds into a food processor or blender and process until the nuts are finely ground. Add the olive oil and mix until smooth.
2 Transfer to a small bowl and stir in the chopped almonds.
3 Spread liberally onto each slice of bread.

SERVES 2

PREPARATION
5 minutes

STORAGE
Keep up to a month in an airtight container.

TRY THIS WITH...
apple wedges for a really tasty, protein-rich dip.

HIGH IN...
B vitamins, magnesium, omega-6 oils, and zinc.

PROPERTIES
Almonds are naturally sweet nuts and so they are great for reducing sweet cravings and preventing your children from reaching for a chocolate snack.

morning muesli

SERVES 2

PREPARATION
5 minutes

STORAGE
You can store the muesli in an airtight container up to a month.

TRY THIS WITH...
plain yogurt, as a topping for fruit desserts, or serve with coconut milk.

HIGH IN...
B vitamins, iron, magnesium, omega-3 and -6 oils, and zinc.

PROPERTIES
Pumpkin seeds have fantastic anti-inflammatory properties, which help to address and prevent common childhood conditions, such as eczema, asthma, and acne.

This is so simple to make and so much healthier than muesli from a store. It is an ideal recipe for late-night and midday snacks, as well as for breakfast, and has enough natural sweetness to appeal to younger tastes. You can really involve the kids with this one, too. Get them to make their own, experimenting with the ingredients, which are all dry and so won't make any sticky mess!

⅓ cup dried apricots
⅓ cup dried prunes
⅓ cup hazelnuts
⅓ cup pumpkin seeds
1 cup granola
1 cup rolled oats

1 Roughly chop the apricots and prunes.

2 Place in a large mixing bowl and add all the other ingredients.

3 Mix well, then serve in smaller bowls, adding milk as required.

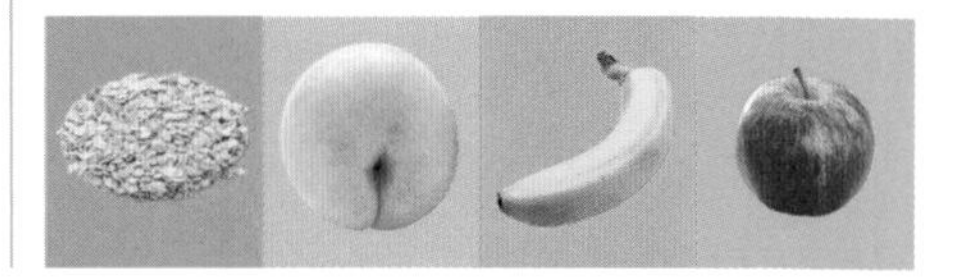

super fruit smoothie

Smoothies are a great way to start the day and you will soon have the whole family demanding them every morning! This recipe packs protein, vitamins, and essential fatty acids into a delicious fruity flavor. We have included flax seed oil, one of the best essential oils, as a supplement for increased brain power and new cell production. You can easily disguise the flavor in a fruit concoction.

1 apple, cored and chopped
1⅓ cups frozen summer fruits
1 banana, chopped
1 avocado, peeled, pitted, and chopped
2 tablespoons flax seed oil
1½ cups unsweetened apple juice
2 tablespoons ground almonds
juice of ½ lime
½ lime, cut into slices

1 Place the apple in a blender. Add all the other ingredients except the lime slices and blend until smooth.
2 Pour the smoothie mixture into two glasses.
3 Decorate each glass with a slice of lime.

SERVES 2

PREPARATION
10 minutes

STORAGE
You can keep the smoothie in the refrigerator for up to 12 hours.

TRY THIS WITH...
fresh nectarines and strawberries instead of frozen summer fruits.

HIGH IN...
omega-3 and -6 oils, potassium and vitamins C and E.

PROPERTIES
Avocados contain lutein and carotene, both plant nutrients that support the health of your child's eyes.

V

blueberry & apple muffins

HIGH IN...
anthocyanidins, fibre and vitamin C.

PROPERTIES
Blueberries are packed full of anthocyanidins, the natural chemicals that give this fruit its intense color. They have been shown to improve brain function, including memory.

The blueberries in these handy breakfast muffins gives your child a good dose of anthocyanidins, the red–blue pigment that increases blood circulation to the brain, promoting good memory, mental acuity, and learning capacity.

Blueberries are highly rated in scientific studies, showing they have the best antioxidant protection (see page 15) for your child's growing brain.

1 stick butter, softened
¼ cup packed light brown sugar
2 eggs, beaten
½ teaspoon cinnamon
2 tablespoons orange marmalade
grated peel of 1 orange
1 cup self-rising flour
1¼ cup rolled oats
1 apple, cored and grated with skin
¾ cup blueberries

1 Preheat the oven to 400°F. Cream together the butter and sugar. Slowly stir in the eggs, cinnamon, marmalade and orange peel.
2 Add the flour and oats, beating together the batter until smooth. Gently stir in the apple and blueberries.
3 Divide the batter between 12 muffin cups, filling each about two-thirds of the way. Bake in the oven 20 to 30 minutes until golden brown.
4 Transfer to a wire rack and leave to cool.

MAKES 12 MUFFINS

PREPARATION + COOKING
10 + 30 minutes

STORAGE
You can keep the cooked muffins up to a week in an airtight container.

TRY THIS WITH...
bananas instead of blueberries, for variety.

If your child is allergic to wheat, use a gluten-free flour for this recipe.

V

sweet quinoa

SERVES 2

PREPARATION
20 minutes

STORAGE
Refrigerate 24 hours and reheat in a microwave or over low heat on the stovetop.

TRY THIS WITH...
chopped bananas or strawberries on top.

HIGH IN...
B vitamins, calcium, and protein.

PROPERTIES
Cinnamon is a great natural sweetener, which acts like the hormone insulin in the body, helping to balance your child's blood sugar.

Quinoa has a delicious nutty taste and a chewy texture kids love. It is a complete protein, meaning that it contains all the amino acids we need for body and brain health—its overall health-giving properties are probably why the Peruvian Incas called it "Mother Grain." Today, as its nutritional value becomes increasingly clear, we use quinoa more and more as an alternative to oatmeal.

1½ cups water
⅔ cup quinoa
½ cup milk, plus extra to serve (optional)
1 teaspoon cinnamon
brown sugar, to serve (optional)

1 Pour the water into a small saucepan, add the quinoa, and leave to simmer over low heat 15 minutes, stirring occasionally.

2 When mixture is thick, add the milk, and stir over low heat 2 minutes longer.

3 Remove the pan from the heat. Add the cinnamon to the quinoa and stir. Pour into bowls. Add extra milk to cool, or brown sugar to sweeten, if absolutely necessary.

007

breakfast kabobs

Eggs are a complete protein (see opposite) and a compact fuel source for the day ahead, providing a mix of B vitamins and minerals, which make them almost the perfect foodstuff. They really fill up kids' tummies and keep them energized right throughout the morning.

16 cherry tomatoes
16 button mushrooms
4 eggs
2 tablespoons chopped parsley

1 Skewer 4 tomatoes and 4 mushrooms alternately onto a kabob skewer, and repeat until you have used all the tomatoes and mushrooms (making 4 kabobs).

2 Place the kabobs under a hot broiler and broil for 10 minutes, or until light brown.

3 Crack the eggs into a poacher and poach for 4 to 6 minutes. Serve the kabobs alongside the poached eggs, sprinkled with chopped parsley.

SERVES 2

PREPARATION + COOKING
5 + 10 minutes

STORAGE
Eat immediately.

TRY THIS WITH...
a side dish of Baked Bean Melt (see page 51).

HIGH IN...
B vitamins, lycopene, manganese, protein, selenium, and zinc.

PROPERTIES
Eggs are a very good source of tryptophan, which we need to make the feel-good brain chemical serotonin.

prune & apricot yogurt

Yogurts don't have to be packed with sugar to taste sweet and delicious. Prunes and apricots provide just the right level of natural sweetness, but don't send blood-sugar levels soaring, and then inevitably crashing again shortly afterward.

SERVES 2

PREPARATION
5 minutes

STORAGE
Keep in the refrigerator up to 2 days.

TRY THIS WITH...
fresh fruit, such as bananas or strawberries.

HIGH IN...
antioxidants, beneficial bacteria, calcium, fiber, and manganese.

PROPERTIES
Prunes are known to have one of the highest levels of antioxidants, beating even broccoli and blueberries. They are also high in soluble and insoluble fiber, that both keep digestion working and clear out toxins.

⅓ cup dried prunes
⅓ cup dried apricots
¾ cup granola
¾ cup plain yogurt with live cultures
2 tablespoons sunflower seeds

1 Roughly chop the prunes and apricots.

2 Mix the prunes, apricots, granola, and yogurt in a large bowl. Divide between two dishes and sprinkle with the sunflower seeds.

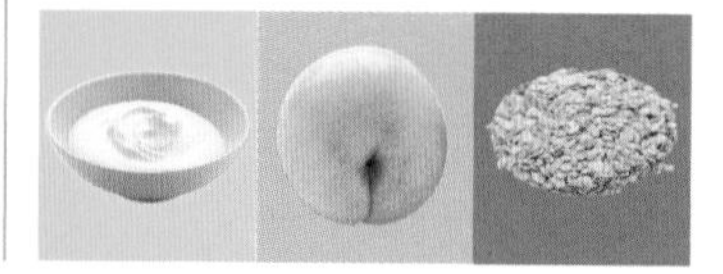

crunchy oatmeal

A great twist on an old favorite, this dish provides all the nutrients for good moods and increased alertness. The seeds are both creamy and crunchy and really add to the texture of a food that provides solid fuel to keep energy levels high throughout the day.

1¼ cups rolled oats
1¼ cups soymilk
1 tablespoon molasses or brown sugar
2 tablespoons sunflower seeds
2 tablespoons pumpkin seeds

1 Pour the oats and soymilk into a saucepan over medium heat. Alternatively, pour the milk and oats into a bowl and cook 5 to 7 minutes in a microwave.

2 Bring to a boil, stirring regularly; or remove from the microwave after 3 minutes, stir, and return to the microwave 2 to 4 minutes longer.

3 When the mixture is slightly thicker, add the molasses or sugar, and stir. Remove the pan from the heat, spoon the oatmeal into individual bowls, and sprinkle with the seeds.

SERVES 2

PREPARATION + COOKING
2 + 10 minutes

STORAGE
Refrigerate up to 6 hours and reheat in a microwave or over low heat.

TRY THIS WITH...
fresh fruit, such as bananas, strawberries, or dried prunes.

HIGH IN...
B vitamins, calcium, fiber, magnesium, omega-6 oils, and zinc.

PROPERTIES
Sunflower and pumpkin seeds provide plenty of omega-6 oils to boost brain power, and molasses provides a wonderful good-mood food.

banana & buckwheat crêpes

HIGH IN...
calcium, omega-6 oils, potassium, and vitamins B6 and B12.

PROPERTIES
Buckwheat has been shown to significantly lower blood sugar and is recommended for the dietary management of diabetes.

Buckwheat is not related to wheat and makes a perfect alternative, as it has more leveling effects on blood sugar. Therefore, as a breakfast food, it sends your child to school more able to focus, stay calm, and have energy right up until lunchtime.

Buckwheat also has a high capacity to satisfy hunger, so it can reduce the likelihood of sugary snack cravings. Both buckwheat and bananas are good sources of the B vitamins that are so vital for mental activity and brain power.

2 eggs
1¾ cups buckwheat flour
1½ cups milk
2 large bananas, sliced
½ cup slivered almonds, toasted
maple syrup, to serve

1 Sift the flour into a mixing bowl. Add the eggs and milk and whisk together until smooth, adding a little extra milk, if necessary. Leave in the refrigerator 30 minutes.

2 Wipe a large skillet with oil and heat. When hot, pour in 2 tablespoons batter and tip the pan so the batter covers the bottom. Cook the crêpe on both sides until light brown. Repeat until all the batter is used.

3 Serve each crêpe with the banana slices, a sprinkle of almonds, and a drizzle of maple syrup.

MAKES 6 TO 10 PANCAKES

PREPARATION + COOKING
35 + 10 minutes

STORAGE
You can refrigerate the crêpe batter up to 3 days.

TRY THIS WITH...
plain yogurt with live cultures for the added benefit of good bacteria.

To make these lower in sugar, use local honey or manuka honey from New Zealand in place of the maple syrup.

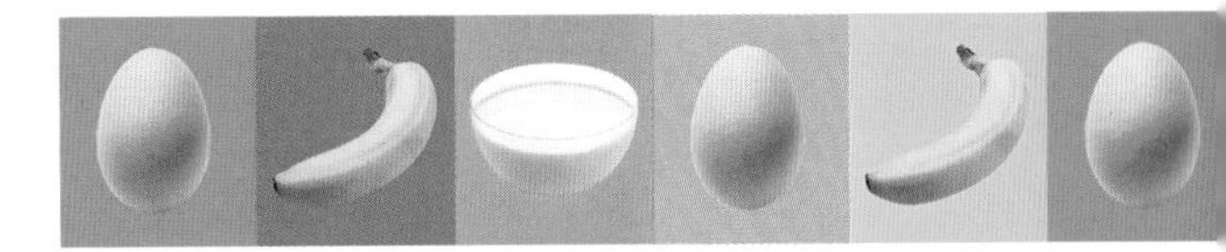

asparagus egg scramble

SERVES 2

PREPARATION + COOKING
5 + 10 minutes

STORAGE
You can refrigerate a few hours and serve cold.

TRY THIS WITH...
chopped cilantro sprinkled on top, for extra flavor.

HIGH IN...
fiber, folate, protein, and vitamins E and K.

PROPERTIES
Asparagus contains the prebiotic fiber inulin. This feeds the good bacteria in your child's gut, which is crucial for good digestive function and immunity.

Asparagus is a surprisingly useful breakfast food. If vegetables at breakfast are new to your children, introduce them slowly in small quantities and in familiar foods, such as this delicious take on scrambled eggs.

2 tablespoons olive oil
7 ounces asparagus, trimmed and finely chopped
4 eggs
¼ cup milk
¼ teaspoon celery salt
2 tablespoons butter
4 slices rye bread

1 Heat the olive oil in a nonstick saucepan. Add the chopped asparagus and stir-fry gently 3 to 4 minutes.
2 Crack the eggs into a bowl, add the milk, celery salt, and butter, and beat with a fork.
3 Gently heat a second nonstick pan and pour in the egg mixture. Stir continuously over low heat until the liquid begins to congeal, then add the asparagus.
4 Meanwhile, toast the rye bread and spread with butter. Serve the asparagus scramble over the rye bread.

V

mediterranean melts

This recipe's combination of goat cheese and tomatoes is reminiscent of a meal on the Mediterranean, where the healthy diet, rich in the natural foods of the lush environment, has been linked with the prevention of disease throughout life.

2 slices rye bread
3 ounces goat cheese
8 cherry tomatoes
2 tablespoons chopped basil

1 Heat the broiler to medium. Spread the slices of rye bread with the goat cheese. Chop the cherry tomatoes in half and arrange them equally over the tops.
2 Broil 5 to 10 minutes until the cheese melts.
3 Remove from the broiler and sprinkle with the basil before serving.

SERVES 2

PREPARATION + COOKING
5 + 10 minutes

STORAGE
Refrigerate up to a day.

TRY THIS WITH...
a glass of Rejuvenating Juice (see page 24).

HIGH IN...
B vitamins, fiber, lycopene, and vitamins A and C.

PROPERTIES
Rye is a valuable source of fiber, which is often missing from children's diets. Lycopene is the plant chemical that gives tomatoes their red color and provides a high dose of antioxidants.

hummus & rye toasts

SERVES 2

PREPARATION
5 minutes

STORAGE
You can refrigerate overnight and eat the following morning.

TRY THIS WITH...
avocado added to the hummus for a breakfast rich in vitamin E.

HIGH IN...
B vitamins, calcium, fiber, manganese, magnesium, and vitamin C.

PROPERTIES
Red bell pepper has three times as much vitamin C as an equivalently sized orange! Alfalfa sprouts are high in the enzymes that help good digestion and clear out toxins from the body.

Hummus might seem an unusual choice for breakfast, yet we in the West are actually the unusual ones. Elsewhere in the world people often eat savory rather than sweet food for breakfast. This recipe is a great alternative to "empty-calorie" breakfast options, such as sweet and processed cereals, we so often give our children.

4 slices rye bread
4 tablespoons hummus
2 handfuls alfalfa sprouts
1 red bell pepper, seeded and thinly sliced

1 Toast the slices of rye bread. Spread each slice liberally with the hummus.

2 Sprinkle half a handful of alfalfa sprouts over the hummus.

3 Top with the red peppers.

creamed salmon rice cakes

Rice cakes are a great, easy alternative to bread and wheat options. Kids love their nutty taste and popcornlike texture. They are the perfect blank canvas for any topping and easy to make for those hectic, "late-for-school-again" moments!

1 avocado
½ cup chopped spinach
2 tablespoons chopped cilantro
2 ounces smoked salmon, chopped
2 tablespoons cream cheese
freshly ground black pepper
lemon wedge
4 plain rice cakes (no salt added)
4 sprigs parsley

1 Scoop the avocado flesh into a small mixing bowl. Add the chopped spinach, cilantro, and salmon, then stir in the cream cheese.
2 Add some black pepper and squeeze in the juice from the lemon wedge. Stir the mixture well until creamy in texture.
3 Spread each rice cake equally with the mixture, garnish with parsley, and serve.

SERVES 2

PREPARATION
10 minutes

STORAGE
You can refrigerate the topping mixture up to 2 days.

TRY THIS WITH...
rye bread or use as a lunchtime sandwich filling.

HIGH IN...
B vitamins, fiber, magnesium, protein, omega-3 oils, and vitamins A, C, and E.

PROPERTIES
Omega-3 oils in the salmon provide all the right nutrients to increase your child's capacity for learning and development throughout their day.

LUNCHES

A good lunch is essential if your child is to sustain his or her energy level throughout the day. It is therefore vital—in lunchboxes and at home during vacations and over the weekends—that you encourage your child to eat foods rich in good-quality proteins, carbohydrates, and other nutrients to prevent energy lows, bad moods and tiredness. Lunch is also a good time to encourage your child to help in the kitchen, doing simple tasks such as stirring ingredients, and washing, peeling, and, most importantly, tasting healthy raw ingredients such as carrots, tomatoes, and cheese. They can then sample the cooked dishes to discover how the flavors have developed. He or she will soon become a master chef, purely by osmosis!

broccoli & almond soup

Both broccoli and almonds are recognized as superfoods—they contain a wealth of immune-boosting nutrients, including the antioxidant vitamins C and E, which have been proven to ward off diseases. They also support a healthy digestive system.

SERVES 4

PREPARATION + COOKING
5 + 20 minutes

STORAGE
You can refrigerate up to 3 days or freeze and use within a month.

TRY THIS...
cold or use as a sauce for white fish or other vegetables.

HIGH IN...
B vitamins, fiber, magnesium, sulfurophanes, and zinc.

PROPERTIES
Broccoli contains substances called sulfurophanes, which have been shown to significantly help the liver remove toxins and support the immune system.

1 tablespoon olive oil
1 onion, diced
1 quart water
4 teaspoons vegetable bouillon powder
heaped ¾ cup whole almonds
1½ cups broccoli flowerets

1 Heat the oil in a medium saucepan. Add the onion and gently fry until golden. Add the water, bouillon powder, almonds, and broccoli flowerets.

2 Simmer 10 minutes, then remove from the heat and leave to cool 5 minutes. Pour the mixture into a blender, give it a whiz, and then serve in individual bowls.

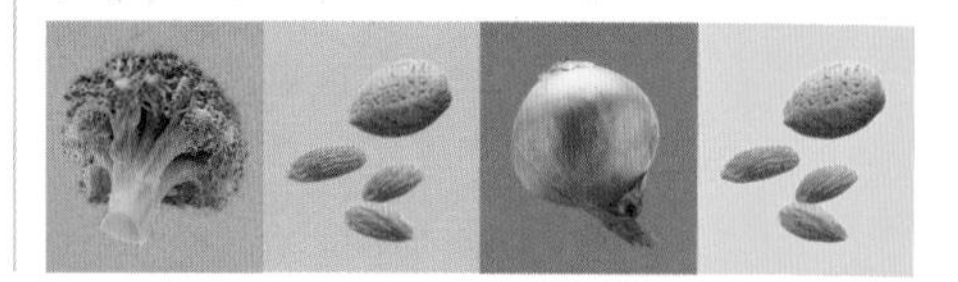

steamy chicken soup

Lower in saturated fats than other meats and high in easily absorbed proteins, chicken also contains a host of B vitamins essential for good mood. Numerous studies have even shown that chicken soup is a perfect food for children recovering from illness. Furthermore, soup is a brilliant way to hide vegetables, and it provides a solid, warming source of fuel, especially on a cold day.

1 tablespoon olive oil
2 cups roughly chopped skinless chicken breast
1 onion, diced
1 garlic clove, crushed
1 quart water
4 teaspoons vegetable bouillon powder
1 can (28-oz) corn kernels, drained

1 Heat the oil in a wok or large skillet. Add the chicken and cook until light brown. Then add the onion and garlic and sauté 1 to 2 minutes longer.

2 Add the water, bouillon powder, and corn, and simmer 10 minutes, until the chicken is cooked through. Remove the pan from heat and leave the soup to cool 5 minutes.

3 Pour the soup into a blender and process until smooth. Return to the pan to reheat, then serve.

SERVES 4

PREPARATION + COOKING
5 + 20 minutes

STORAGE
You can refrigerate for up to 3 days or freeze up to a month.

TRY THIS WITH...
some bread sticks, an apple, and a small bag of prunes to help your child fill up on healthy fiber.

HIGH IN...
selenium, sulfur, tryptophan, and vitamins B3 and B6.

PROPERTIES
The vitamin B3 in chicken is important for stable, happy moods, as it helps to release energy from carbohydrate and encourages good sugar balance.

carrot & parsnip soup

SERVES 4

PREPARATION + COOKING
10 + 15 minutes

STORAGE
You can refrigerate up to 3 days or freeze 1 month.

TRY THIS WITH...
some crunchy rye-bread croutons.

HIGH IN...
beta-carotene and vitamins A and K.

PROPERTIES
The rich orange color of carrots comes from their high levels of the antioxidant beta-carotene, which protects the eyes—hence the saying that carrots help you to see in the dark.

Carrot soup is always a sweet favorite with kids. Presenting carrots in liquid form enables their health-giving beta-carotene to get straight into your child's digestive tract, where it can help support digestion and immunity.

1 tablespoon olive oil
1 onion, diced
1 teaspoon coriander seeds
4 carrots, peeled and sliced
4 parsnips, peeled and sliced
1 teaspoon ground cinnamon
2 cups water
1 tablespoon vegetable bouillon powder
2 tablespoons chopped parsley

1 Heat the oil in a saucepan. Add the onion and sauté until light brown.

2 Add the coriander seeds, carrots, parsnips, cinnamon, water, and bouillon powder. Simmer 15 minutes, or until the vegetables are soft.

3 Pour the soup into a blender and process until smooth. Pour into individual bowls and garnish each with a sprinkle of parsley.

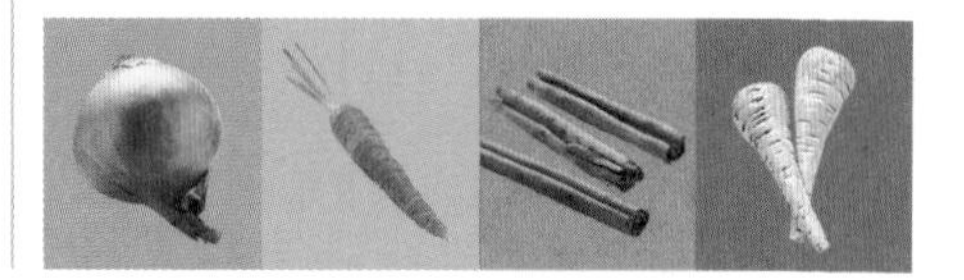

potato & lentil burgers

You'll find everyone will love the creamy texture of this tasty dish—a great way to disguise those lentils.

1 pound 2 ounces Idaho potatoes
heaped ½ cup red lentils
1 tablespoon olive oil
1 small onion, diced
1 garlic clove, crushed
1 egg, beaten
2 tablespoons finely chopped chives
½ cup grated cheddar cheese

1 Half fill a saucepan with water and bring to a boil. Add the potatoes, cover, and leave to simmer 15 to 20 minutes until soft. Drain and then mash. Meanwhile, in a separate pan, simmer the lentils 15 to 20 minutes, or until tender, then drain. Heat the oil in a small saucepan. Add the onion and garlic and fry until golden.

2 Heat the oven to 425°F. In a large mixing bowl, mix the mashed potatoes, lentils, onion mixture, egg, chives, and cheese. Use your hands to shape the mixture into 12 burgers and place on a nonstick baking sheet.

3 Put the burgers in the oven and bake for 20 minutes, or until golden. Serve immediately.

SERVES 4

PREPARATION + COOKING
10 + 40 minutes

STORAGE
You can freeze the unbaked burgers to use within a month.

TRY THIS WITH...
a green salad, peas, and sour cream and chive dip, or salsa.

HIGH IN...
B vitamins, fiber and sulfur.

PROPERTIES
The mineral sulfur, found in the lentils, eggs, and onions in this recipe, helps to clear toxins from your child's body and aid new skin growth.

chicken noodle nest

SERVES 4

PREPARATION + COOKING
10 + 5 minutes

STORAGE
You can refrigerate up to a day and then reheat.

TRY THIS WITH...
coconut milk for a sweeter Thai flavor your child will love!

HIGH IN...
bioflavonoids, magnesium, vitamins C and E, and zinc.

PROPERTIES
Tamari offers the benefits of traditionally fermented forms of soy, without the wheat content of other soy sauces.

Kids love the sweet flavors of the vegetables in this dish. Even if they pick out a few things, they'll still absorb a variety of nutrients to keep them happy and focused until bedtime.

1 tablespoon olive oil
2 boneless chicken breast halves, about 5 ounces each
1 teaspoon chopped gingerroot
¾ cup snow peas
scant 1/½ cups chopped green cabbage
4 ounces udon noodles
1 stick lemongrass, sliced
6 scallions, chopped
2 star anise, chopped
3 tablespoons bottled sweet chili sauce
3 tablespoons tamari soy sauce
2 tablespoons chopped cilantro

1 Heat the oil in a wok. Add the chicken and fry lightly until cooked through. Then add the ginger, snow peas, cabbage, noodles, and lemongrass and stir-fry 2 to 3 minutes.

2 Add the scallions, star anise, and sauces and fry another minute. If mixture is too dry, add extra tamari.

3 Remove from the heat and serve on plates sprinkled with the chopped cilantro.

salmon & cilantro fishcakes

Fishcakes make a really healthy alternative to hamburgers. Rich in carbohydrate and protein, they will energize your child all afternoon long.

1 pound 2 ounces Idaho potatoes, peeled and chopped
4 salmon steaks, about 3 ounces each
1 tablespoon olive oil
4 scallions, chopped
1 leek, trimmed and sliced
3 tablespoon wholegrain mustard
1 tablespoon bottled sweet chili sauce, plus extra for serving

1 Half fill a saucepan with water and bring to a boil. Add the potatoes, cover, and leave to simmer 15 to 20 minutes until soft. Drain and mash. Cook the salmon steaks under a medium broiler 10 minutes, turning twice. When cooked, remove any skin and break into flakes.

2 Heat the oven to 425°F. Heat the oil in a skillet. Add the scallions and leek and fry 3 minutes until soft. Stir these into the mashed potatoes, together with the salmon, mustard, and chili sauce.

3 Use your hands to shape the mixture into 8 fishcakes and place on a nonstick baking sheet. Put in the oven and cook for 20 minutes, or until golden brown. Remove and serve with extra sweet chili sauce.

SERVES 4

PREPARATION + COOKING
5 + 50 minutes

STORAGE
You can freeze the unbaked fishcakes to use within a month.

TRY THIS WITH...
peas, an arugula salad, and (if your child likes spicy foods) tartar or horseradish sauce.

HIGH IN...
fiber and omega-3 oils; healthy, brain-boosting monounsaturated fats.

PROPERTIES
The fish oils in this recipe help to support the healing of inflammatory conditions such as eczema, acne, psoriasis, and asthma.

peach & prosciutto salad

HIGH IN...
beta-carotene, iron, lycopene, protein, and silica.

PROPERTIES
Cucumber contains silica, a mineral that helps plants to stand up. In humans, silica is an essential component of healthy skin.

Using fruit in savory dishes is something many children really love. The combination of many differently colored fruits and vegetables provides a wealth of antioxidants to protect a growing body from free radicals—harmful by-products of cell metabolism triggered by such things as pollution, emissions from computers and TVs, and life's stresses, generally. In addition, superfood spinach has been shown to improve motor skills and learning capacity.

4 peaches with skins, cut into thirds and pits removed
12 slices prosciutto
1½ cups chopped snow peas
4 cups chopped baby spinach
1 red onion, sliced
4 ounces cherry or baby plum tomatoes, cut in half
½ cucumber, grated
3 tablespoons olive oil
1 tablespoon balsamic vinegar
4 sprigs mint

1 Heat the broiler to medium. Wrap a slice of prosciutto around each peach piece and place on a broiler pan. Broil 3 to 6 minutes until light brown.
2 Meanwhile, place the snow peas and spinach in a salad bowl. Add the red onion, tomatoes, and cucumber and stir together, adding the olive oil and balsamic vinegar.
3 Divide the salad equally between four plates. Place three of the peach and prosciutto wraps alongside each salad and garnish with a sprig of mint.

SERVES 4

PREPARATION + COOKING
10 + 6 minutes

STORAGE
You can store the salad up to 24 hours in the refrigerator.

TRY THIS WITH...
wholewheat, rye, or mixed-grain bread for extra fiber.

If your child is under 4 years old, replace the prosciutto with bacon, which is less salty.

mexican beanfeast

Here is a healthier alternative to the traditional chili con carne. The beans are full of fiber and plant protein, rather than the saturated fat you get in the traditional beef version.

SERVES 4

PREPARATION + COOKING
5 + 20 minutes

STORAGE
You can refrigerate up to 3 days or freeze and use within a month.

TRY THIS WITH...
grated cheese, hummus, or sour cream on the side, or serve with brown rice.

HIGH IN...
calcium, fiber, lycopene, magnesium, and protein.

PROPERTIES
Cooked tomatoes provide higher levels of the antioxidant compound lycopene, which gives tomatoes their red color, and protects children's eyes, heart, and skin.

1 tablespoon olive oil
1 small red onion, diced
2 teaspoons chili powder
1 teaspoon cayenne pepper
2 tablespoons Worcestershire sauce
1⅓ cups tomato paste
½ red bell pepper, seeded and sliced
1 can (7-oz) whole corn kernels
1 can (15-oz) kidney beans, drained
1 can (15-oz) chickpeas, drained
1 can (28-oz) crushed tomatoes
4 wholewheat pita breads
3 tablespoons instant gravy mix
1 bunch scallions, chopped
2 tablespoons chopped parsley

1 Heat the oil in a wok. Add the onion and fry until light brown, then stir in the chili powder, cayenne pepper, Worcestershire sauce, and tomato paste.

2 Add the red pepper, corn, kidney beans, chickpeas, and crushed tomatoes and simmer 10 minutes. Meanwhile, toast the pitas lightly under a hot broiler. Remove from the heat and cut in half to make two pockets.

3 Add the instant gravy to the beanfeast, and stir well, then simmer 5 minutes. Add the scallions and parsley and serve in individual bowls with the pitas on the side.

V

baked bean melt

This homemade version of a canned favorite contains far less sugar, and is a rich source of mood-enhancing tryptophan.

5½ tablespoons vegetable oil
1 small onion, diced
3 garlic cloves, crushed
1 red bell pepper, seeded and chopped
1 cup water
¾ cup maple syrup
1⅓ cups tomato paste
2 tablespoons blackstrap molasses
2 tablespoons apple cider vinegar
1 teaspoon Dijon mustard
½ teaspoon freshly ground black pepper
1 can (15-oz) cooked pinto beans, drained
4 slices wholewheat bread
1¼ cups grated cheddar cheese

1 Heat the oven to 325°F. Heat the oil in a large saucepan. Add the onion, garlic, and red pepper and fry for several minutes, then set aside.

2 In a large bowl, whisk together the water, maple syrup, tomato paste, molasses, vinegar, mustard, and pepper. Add the beans and pepper mixture and stir together. Pour into a large, shallow baking dish, cover, tightly, and bake 30 minutes. If necessary, add extra water to preserve the liquid content.

3 Lightly toast the bread. Spoon the cooked beans over the bread and serve sprinkled with the grated cheese.

SERVES 2

PREPARATION + COOKING
10 + 30 minutes

STORAGE
Store leftover baked beans in the refrigerator up to 3 days.

TRY THIS WITH...
a baked potato for a snack packed with fiber.

HIGH IN...
fiber, folate, manganese, and tryptophan.

PROPERTIES
Garlic contains detoxifying sulfur and is also a potent antibiotic, so it can help ward off infections.

V

vegetable lasagne

This heartwarming lasagne provides all the vital nutrients for health and happiness.

SERVES 4

PREPARATION + COOKING
5 + 40 minutes

STORAGE
Once cooked, refrigerate up to 3 days, then reheat. You can freeze the raw dish up to a month.

TRY THIS WITH...
a light green salad, spinach, or homemade garlic bread.

HIGH IN...
lutein, lycopene, omega-6 oils, selenium, and vitamin E.

PROPERTIES
Mushrooms are high in the immune-supporting mineral selenium; those from organic soils provide the best levels.

2 tablespoons olive oil
1 onion, diced
2 garlic cloves, sliced
1 red bell pepper, seeded and sliced
1⅔ cups sliced mushrooms
1⅓ cups chopped green cabbage
1 handful sunflower seeds
1 handful pumpkin seeds
1 teaspoon celery salt
1 teaspoon cinnamon
⅔ cup tomato paste
1 tablespoon bottled sweet chilli sauce
1 can (15-oz) chickpeas, drained
1 can (28-oz) crushed tomatoes
2 tablespoons chopped basil
10 sheets no-pre-cook lasagne
7 ounces feta cheese
1 tablespoon butter
1 tablespoon all-purpose flour
scant 2 cups milk
1 cup grated cheddar cheese

1 Heat the oven to 375°F. In a wok, heat the oil. Add the onion, garlic, pepper, mushrooms, and cabbage. and stir-fry over medium-high heat until soft but still bright in color.
2 In a mixing bowl, stir in the next nine ingredients, then add the wok mixture. Spread half in a baking dish and crumble half the feta over. Cover with half the lasagne, then the rest of the feta. Layer with tomato mix and lasagne
3 Melt the butter in a pan, add the flour, then stir in the milk. Add the cheese, stir until thick, then pour it over the lasagne. Cook for 30 minutes.

bean cassoulet

This mix of healthy beans can help combat any digestive and skin complaints. Cook them slowly to break down the hard-to-digest fiber, which can cause wind or bloating. If either of these is a problem, add a piece of seaweed (from health-food stores) to the cooking water to help with the fiber breakdown.

heaped ½ cup dry haricot beans
heaped ½ cup dry mung beans
heaped ½ cup dry lima beans
1 quart water
4 teaspoons vegetable bouillon powder
2½ cups sliced mushrooms
1 can (15-oz) crushed tomatoes
3 garlic cloves, sliced
2 stalks celery, sliced
4 tablespoons tomato paste
8 shallots
5 tablespoons olive oil
1 teaspoon oregano
4 sprigs basil

1 Soak all the beans in water overnight.

2 Heat the oven to 375°F. Drain the beans and pour them into a large ovenproof dish with a tight-fitting lid. Add the remaining ingredients, except the basil, and stir well.

3 Cover the dish and place in the oven 40 to 50 minutes, stirring every 20 minutes. Remove and serve on plates, garnished with the basil.

SERVES 4

PREPARATION + COOKING
overnight soak +10 + 50 minutes

STORAGE
You can refrigerate up to 3 days, or freeze and then reheat within a month.

TRY THIS AS...
a filling for baked potatoes with a sprinkling of grated cheese.

HIGH IN...
B vitamins, calcium, fiber, magnesium, protein, and tryptophan.

PROPERTIES
These three types of beans provide lots of different proteins to support neurotransmitter production, including feel-good serotonin, which the body makes from tryptophan.

brunch bonanza

Sausages can have health benefits if you choose them carefully. Go to a butcher you trust, buy organic, and check labels to insure they contain real ground meat rather than mechanically reconstituted meat (MRM), and are not packed with fillers.

SERVES 4

PREPARATION + COOKING
10 + 30 minutes

STORAGE
Eat this dish on the same day you cook it.

TRY THIS WITH...
a salad and toasted rye bread for extra energy on a cold day.

HIGH IN...
beta-carotene, iron, lycopene, selenium, and sulfur.

PROPERTIES
The body absorbs iron from meat much more easily than iron from plant sources. Your child's body uses iron to fully oxygenate his or her blood and create energy. If the sausages are made from lean meat, such as turkey or lamb, rather than pork, they will be a richer source of protein and iron.

1⅔ cups sliced mushrooms
16 cherry tomatoes, cut in half
1 onion, diced
2 garlic cloves, thinly sliced
2 leeks, trimmed and sliced
2 sweet potatoes, peeled and chopped
8 link sausages, sliced
3 to 4 tablespoons olive oil
2 tablespoons chopped parsley

1 Heat the oven to 375°F. Scatter the mushrooms and cherry tomatoes into a medium baking dish. Add the onion, garlic, leek, sweet potatoes, and sausages.

2 Drizzle the olive oil over and sprinkle with the parsley. Bake in the oven 20 to 30 minutes until the sweet potatoes are soft. Remove from the oven and serve hot.

V

great greens "risotto"

Do not underestimate the power of "green foods." The body unlocks the energy potential of chlorophyll—which creates the green colour in plants—to fuel growth and the ability to cope with new situations.

1 quart water
4 teaspoons vegetable bouillon powder
heaped 1 cup risotto rice
2 tablespoons sesame oil
2 garlic cloves
1 cup broccoli flowerets
1¼ cups chopped asparagus
1½ cups chopped snowpeas
2 apples, grated
3 tablespoons pumpkin seeds
1 sprig rosemary
1 cup grated cheddar cheese
freshly ground black pepper

1 Pour the water into a saucepan and add the bouillon powder and rice. Bring to a boil, then cover and simmer 15 minutes, stirring occasionally, until the rice absorbs all the water. Remove the pan from the heat.

2 Heat the sesame oil in a wok. Add the garlic, broccoli, asparagus, and snow peas and stir-fry 2 to 3 minutes until tender. Add the apple, pumpkin seeds, rosemary, and risotto rice and stir.

3 If necessary, add a little more water for a smooth but sticky consistency. Serve on individual plates, sprinkled with the grated cheese and black pepper.

SERVES 4

PREPARATION + COOKING
10 + 20 minutes

STORAGE
Ideally, eat the risotto fresh, but you can store it overnight in a refrigerator and then reheat it.

TRY THIS WITH...
an arugula salad or add some chicken for a meatier dish.

HIGH IN...
B vitamins, calcium, fiber, and magnesium.

PROPERTIES
Fiber helps to normalize digestion, feed your child's healthy, immune-supporting gut bacteria, and remove harmful toxins from their body.

feisty fiesta pizza

SERVES 4

PREPARATION + COOKING
15 + 20 minutes

STORAGE
You can freeze the pizza dough up to a month, or refrigerate the cooked pizza overnight and eat it cold for breakfast or lunch!

TRY THIS WITH...
Bright Bean Salad
(see page 93).

HIGH IN...
fiber, lycopene, selenium, and vitamin C.

PROPERTIES
Gram flour is made from chickpeas and is a great source of fiber and a healthy alternative to wheat flour.

Pizza, a real favorite with most children, is usually an unhealthy choice. But, if oven-baked and made with choice ingredients, this junk food can become a health food.

½ teaspoon dried yeast
1 cup warm water
1 teaspoon brown sugar
heaped ¾ cup gram flour
¾ cup cornstarch
1½ tablespoons olive oil
1 teaspoon chili powder
1 teaspoon celery salt
¾ cup tomato paste
½ red bell pepper, seeded and sliced
½ yellow bell pepper, seeded and sliced
⅔ cup mushrooms
¾ cup grated cheddar cheese

1 Heat the oven to 425°F. In a small bowl, dissolve the yeast in half the warm water, add the sugar, mix well, and set aside 15 minutes.

2 Place the flour in a bowl, add the yeast mixture, cornstarch, olive oil, chili powder, and celery salt and beat with a wooden spoon. Add the remaining warm water, a little at a time, beating until the consistency is thick. Once thick enough, remove the dough and knead.

3 Spread the dough out flat onto a nonstick baking sheet, then bake at the top of the oven 5 minutes. Remove from the oven and add the tomato paste and toppings, then return to the oven and cook 20 minutes until brown.

sweet potato & spinach curry

A sweet curry that benefits from the inclusion of coconut milk, this recipe provides healthy fats, so it tastes deliciously indulgent.

1 tablespoon olive oil
1 onion, diced
2 garlic cloves, thinly sliced
2 large sweet potatoes, peeled and chopped
½ stick cinnamon
2 teaspoons coriander seeds
1 teaspoon curry powder
2 teaspoons vegetable bouillon powder
1½ cups water
1½ cups brown basmati rice
4 cups chopped spinach
½ cup pumpkin seeds
⅓ cup raisins
1¾ cups coconut milk
2 tablespoons chopped parsley

1 Half fill a large saucepan with wate and bring to a boil. Add the rice, return to a boil, then reduce the heat to low. Cover and leave to simmer 15 minutes.

2 Meanwhile, heat the oil in a separate saucepan. Add the onion and garlic and sauté. Add the sweet potato, cinnamon, coriander seeds, curry powder, bouillon powder and water and simmer 10 minutes.

3 Add the spinach, seeds, raisins, and coconut milk to the curry. Simmer 5 to 10 minutes longer. Remove both pans from the heat, drain the rice. Serve sprinkled with parsley.

SERVES 4

PREPARATION + COOKING
5 + 20 minutes

STORAGE
You can refrigerate the curry up to 3 days, or freeze it up to a month.

TRY THIS AS...
a soup. Just blend the cooked curry mixture for a thick, hearty, healthy soup.

HIGH IN...
beta-carotene, omega-6 oils, and vitamins A and C.

PROPERTIES
Recently, sweet potatoes have been classified as an "anti-diabetic" food because they have been shown to be so successful at stabilizing blood-sugar levels.

fighting-fit fajitas

HIGH IN...
protein, selenium, tryptophan and vitamins B3, B6, and C.

PROPERTIES
Tuna is an excellent source of all the ingredients your child needs to make serotonin and the other neurotransmitters needed for good mental focus at school.

Tuna is a nutrient-dense food, so it's an especially good source of high-quality protein, providing your child with the building blocks for the hormones and neurotransmitters that keep everyone relaxed, receptive, and positive. As a rich source of omega-3 oils, tuna also provides directly the oils EPA and DHA. Our brains are about 60 percent fat, of which EPA and DHA are crucial components for the communication and protection of brain cells.

SERVES 2

PREPARATION
10 minutes

STORAGE
You can store the mixture in the refrigerator up to 3 days.

TRY THIS WITH...
a bag of dried fruit and a couple of sticks of celery with hummus to make a complete lunchbox.

1 can (3-oz) tuna in olive oil, drained
½ cup canned kidney beans, drained
⅓ cup canned corn kernels, drained
2 scallions, chopped
½ red bell pepper, seeded and chopped
2 tablespoons mayonnaise
pinch chili powder
2 cups arugula
2 flour tortillas

1 Place the tuna into a small bowl and mash.

2 Add all the remaining ingredients, except the arugula and tortillas, and stir together well.

3 Lay out the tortillas and place half the arugula in the middle of each one. Top each with half the tuna mixture, then roll tightly into wraps.

Chili powder aids circulation and helps to keep out the cold.

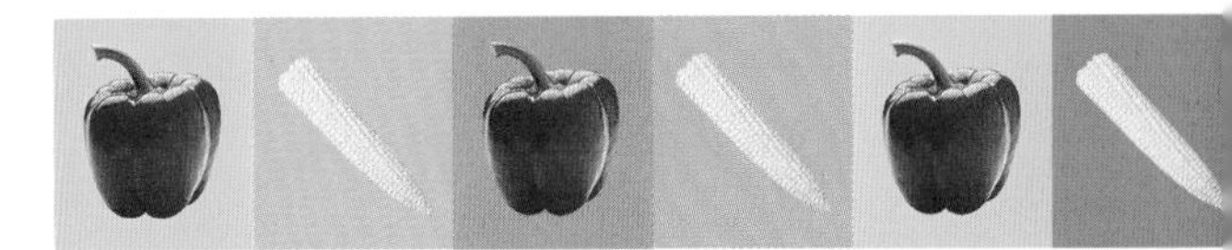

veggie wraps

Soft tortillas are a good alternative to bread and you can even make your own with wheat-free flour; otherwise they are available in most supermarkets or health-food stores. This crunchy filling is a rich source of healthy vegetarian protein, so helps to build the neurotransmitters that insure strong focus throughout the day.

SERVES 2

PREPARATION
10 minutes

STORAGE
You can prepare these the night before and refrigerate until the morning.

TRY THIS WITH...
a small tub of hummus, some raw carrots, and a banana to complete a lunchbox of super-healthy food.

HIGH IN...
B vitamins, fiber, magnesium, tryptophan, and zinc.

PROPERTIES
Alfalfa sprouts contain enzymes that feed the beneficial bacteria in your child's gut, encouraging healthy digestion and protecting against illness.

1 avocado, chopped
2 cups chopped spinach
½ cup alfalfa sprouts
½ cup bean sprouts
⅓ cup pumpkin seeds
3 tablespoons olive oil
1 tablespoon wholegrain mustard
1 tablespoon clear honey
2 flour tortillas

1 Put the avocado and spinach into a mixing bowl. Add the sprouts and seeds.

2 To make the dressing, in a small bowl, whisk together the olive oil, mustard, and honey with a fork. Pour into the avocado and spinach mixture and stir well.

3 Lay out the tortillas and pile half the mixture into the middle of each. Roll tightly into wraps.

V O

bagel burger

Potatoes provide the kind of sustained energy that will get your child through a heavy afternoon at school without energy slumps or loss of concentration. The extra flavors of avocado and salsa are healthy alternatives to catsup, mayo and salad spreads, which are full of unhealthy fats and sugars.

1 wholewheat bagel
⅓ cup arugula
1 potato & lentil burger (see page 45)
1 tablespoon hummus
1 tablespoon salsa (see page 101)
½ avocado, peeled and sliced

1 Cut the bagel in half horizontally and toast lightly. Place the arugula on the bottom half of the bagel and top with the burger.
2 Spread the hummus and salsa on top of the burger and then add the avocado slices.
3 Place the second half of the bagel on top.

SERVES 1

PREPARATION
10 minutes

STORAGE
You can prepare this the night before and refrigerate.

TRY THIS WITH...
any main meal as a good alternative to potatoes, pasta, or rice.

HIGH IN...
antioxidants, fiber, and vitamins B6 and C.

PROPERTIES
Potatoes are surprisingly high in vitamin C and also contain vitamin B6 and potassium to support the immune system.

chicken dippers

SERVES 1

PREPARATION + COOKING
5 + 10 minutes

STORAGE
You can refrigerate the satay sauce up to a month.

TRY THIS WITH...
a Blueberry & Apple Muffin (see pages 28–9) and a bag of mixed pumpkin and sunflower seeds.

HIGH IN...
fiber, folate, manganese, monounsaturated fats, protein, and trytophan.

PROPERTIES
Peanut butter provides a healthy source of monounsaturated fats and fiber, which help to improve cell function and digestion respectively. The protein in peanut butter helps to balance blood-sugar levels.

This is a real favorite! It's easy to prepare and full of the fats necessary for your child's brain development. Be sure to buy peanut butter with no added salt or sugar, which you will find in healthy food aisles in supermarkets or in health-food stores—check the labels.

¼ cup basmati rice
½ teaspoon turmeric
2 tablespoons raisins
1 boneless chicken breast half, about 4 ounces, chopped into cubes
4 tablespoons peanut butter with no added sugar
2 tablespoons olive oil

1 Half fill a small pan with water and bring to a boil. Add the rice, turmeric, and raisins, then cover and simmer 10 minutes, or until the rice is cooked. Drain the rice, let it cool, and place in an airtight container.

2 Meanwhile, heat the broiler to hot. Spear the chicken cubes onto two skewers, brush with half the olive oil, and broil 8 to 10 minutes, turning frequently, until brown.

3 Mix the peanut butter and remaining olive oil with a fork in a small bowl, then pour into a small container. Serve the rice on a plate, topped with the chicken skewers, and put the peanut sauce on the side for dipping into.

pita pockets

Not only is pita bread great for concealing new foods, it is a much healthier alternative to regular bread, which tends to be higher in unhealthy starches and sugar. This vegetarian filling is surprisingly satisfying.

2 wholewheat pitas
½ cup chopped spinach
1 carrot, peeled and grated
1 stalk celery, grated
1 teaspoon coriander seeds
2 tablespoons sunflower seeds
4 tablespoons hummus

1 Toast the pitas lightly under a hot broiler, then slice along the edge of each to create large pockets.
2 Put the spinach, carrot, celery, seeds, and hummus into a bowl and stir together.
3 Spoon the mixture into the pockets.

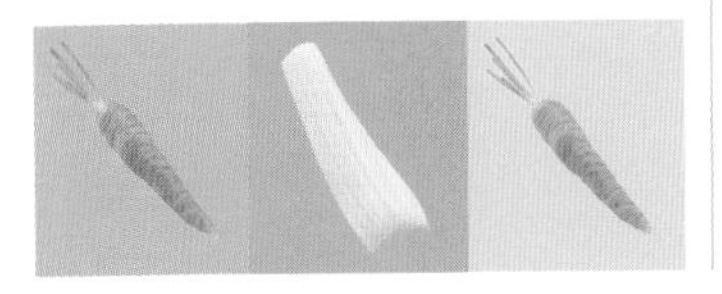

SERVES 2

PREPARATION
10 minutes

STORAGE
You can prepare these the night before and refrigerate them.

TRY THIS WITH...
an apple and Cinnamon Popcorn (see page 78).

HIGH IN...
beta-carotene, potassium, protein, and vitamins A and K.

PROPERTIES
For a leaf, spinach is surprisingly high in protein. With massive quantities of the bone-building vitamins A and K, it is essential for healthy growth.

niçoise wraps

SERVES 4

PREPARATION + COOKING
10 + 10 minutes

STORAGE
You can refrigerate the wrap up to a day. They are great for picnics, too.

TRY THIS WITH...
Sweet Potato Wedges (see pages 72–3).

HIGH IN...
B vitamins, fiber, manganese, monounsaturated fats, and zinc.

PROPERTIES
Lettuce contains good levels of fiber and also of the mineral manganese, which is crucial for blood-sugar regulation.

These tasty wraps give a modern twist to the classic salad. The comforting familiarity of eggs and tuna should gain you the flexibility to add some new and really beneficial ingredients, such as alfalfa sprouts and red onion. The naturally sweet dressing will help to ease the way for the new flavors.

3 eggs
1 red onion, sliced
¾ cup alfalfa sprouts
2 cans (6-oz) tuna in olive oil
1 can (7-oz) corn kernels, drained
2 hearts of lettuce, chopped
3 tablespoons olive oil
1 tablespoon wholegrain mustard
1 tablespoon clear honey
8 flour tortillas

1 Half fill a small saucepan with water and bring to a boil. Gently place in the eggs and boil 8 minutes. Remove from the heat, take out the eggs, and leave them to cool slightly, then break off the shells and slice the eggs.

2 In a mixing bowl, place the egg slices, red onion, alfalfa sprouts, tuna, corn, and lettuce and stir together well.

3 In a small bowl, whisk together the olive oil, mustard, and honey. Pour the tuna mixture over and stir together. Lay out the tortillas and pile the mixture equally into the middle of each and roll tightly into wraps.

fish pâté

Oily fish is a top source of those healthy omega-3 fats your child should eat two or three times a week. This tasty pâté is a great way to provide one portion and is a quick and natural alternative to processed pâtés.

9 ounces boned mackerel fillets, cooked
⅔ cup cream cheese
lemon wedge
2 tablespoons chopped parsley
4 wholewheat bread rolls
butter for spreading
⅔ cup arugula

1 Break up the mackerel fillets into a blender. Add the cream cheese and process until smooth. Squeeze in the lemon juice, add the chopped parsley and stir together.

2 Cut the bread rolls in half and butter the top side. Spread the fish pâté liberally on the bottom halves of the rolls, add one quarter of the arugula to each one, and then close the tops. (Put an extra lemon wedge into your child's lunchbox—if they smear the juice over their fingers after they've eaten it will remove the fishy smell!)

SERVES 4

PREPARATION
10 minutes

STORAGE
You can refrigerate the fish pâté up to 3 days, or freeze it up to a month.

TRY THIS WITH...
snow peas and a Muesli Crunchie (see page 83) for a special treat.

HIGH IN...
antioxidants, calcium, omega-3 oils, and vitamin K.

PROPERTIES
Fresh parsley is one of the highest sources of vitamin K, an often-forgotten nutrient that is crucial for the growth of healthy bones.

DRINKS & SNACKS

Drinks aren't just for hydration—they also provide a good boost of essential vitamins and minerals in an easy-to-absorb form. In addition, making healthy drinks for your children reduces the amount of sugary, commercial drinks they are likely to request. Likewise, snacks aren't just a treat or a filler. If you choose snacks that are low in sugar, added chemicals, and saturated and trans fats, you can make a big difference to your child's health, promoting good blood-sugar balance between meals and boosting essential nutrients.

caribbean cocktail

This is sweet and creamy—a good substitute for ice cream, but with none of the added sugar or saturated fat. The coconut provides plant fats that help to support the immune function and, rather than store them as fat, your child will burn them off as energy, helping to prevent weight problems.

SERVES 4

PREPARATION
10 minutes

STORAGE
Best drunk fresh, but you can refrigerate up to 12 hours.

TRY THIS WITH...
mangoes for extra fiber, flavor, and color!

HIGH IN...
beneficial bacteria, beta-carotene, fiber, manganese, and vitamin C.

PROPERTIES
Pineapple contains a substance called bromelain, which is a natural protein-digester and anti-inflammatory, making it therapeutic for digestive and skin conditions.

1 pineapple
2 bananas
2 cups coconut milk
¾ cup plain yogurt with live cultures
¼ vanilla bean
a little water, if required
4 dried apricots

1 Cut the top and skin off the pineapple. Cut the flesh into chunks, removing the core. Retain four chunks for garnish.
2 Peel the bananas and break into pieces in a blender. Add the pineapple chunks, coconut milk, yogurt, and vanilla bean and process until smooth. Add a little water if the consistency is too thick.
3 Pour the mixture into four glasses. Spear the apricots and reserved pineapple chunks onto toothpicks and place on top of the glasses to serve.

tropical explosion

The bright orange color of this drink shows it is rich in beta-carotene. As the body absorbs liquids more easily than solids, nutrients such as vitamins A and C reach the gut rapidly. Here, they begin their healing work, supporting your child's digestion and helping to alleviate digestive problems.

6 oranges, 1 cut into slices and the rest peeled and flesh chopped
2 mangoes, peeled and chopped
2 passion fruit, seeded and chopped
1 cup apple juice
juice of 1 lime

1 Put the chopped orange flesh, mangoes, and passion fruit into a blender. Add the apple and lime juices and process until smooth.

2 Remove any orange pips and serve in individual glasses decorated with slices of orange.

SERVES 4

PREPARATION
10 minutes

STORAGE
You can refrigerate up to 12 hours.

TRY THIS AS...
a coulis for pouring over desserts—just leave out the apple juice to make it thick.

HIGH IN...
beta-carotene and vitamins A and C.

PROPERTIES
The high antioxidant levels in this drink make it the perfect antidote to pollution damage in the body.

citrus refresher

Your child needs high levels of vitamin C to hit the daily dose required to strengthen immunity and ward off colds and infections. Citrus fruits also contain a potent antioxidant called limonene, which has been shown to be as effective as vitamin C at fighting free radicals and has long-lasting effects when it comes to preventing disease and inflammation.

SERVES 4

PREPARATION + COOKING
10 + 5 minutes + chilling

STORAGE
Refrigerate up to 24 hours.

TRY THIS WITH...
added echinacea drops to fend off more infections.

HIGH IN...
antioxidants and vitamin C.

PROPERTIES
Vitamin C circulates around the body, protecting against damage to cells, tissues, and joints.

8 lemons
2 limes
6 oranges
3 grapefruit
2½ cups water
1 cup packed light brown sugar
ice cubes

1 Grate the peel from a lemon, lime, and orange. Place 1 teaspoon of each peel into a large saucepan. Squeeze the remaining fruit, removing as much juice as possible, then discard the skins.

2 Add the juice to the saucepan and then the water and sugar. Heat gently until the sugar dissolves and leave to simmer 5 minutes.

3 Remove from the heat, leave to cool on the side and then refrigerate at least 4 hours before serving chilled with ice cubes.

spiced apple tea

Spiced apple tea bags are easy to find in any good supermarket or health-food store. Fruit teas make lovely alternatives to sweet drinks and taste great chilled. This drink has a really refreshing taste, but you can vary the fruit tea according to your child's preference.

2 sticks cinnamon
1 lemon, sliced
4 spiced apple tea bags
1 quart boiling water
1 apple, cored and sliced
½ cup frozen cranberries
ice cubes, optional

1 Place the cinnamon sticks, lemon slices, and tea bags in a large heatproof pitcher. Add the boiling water and allow to steep for 30 minutes.
2 Remove the tea bags, then place the spiced tea in the refrigerator overnight.
3 Just before serving, add the apple, frozen cranberries, and ice cubes, if desired. Serve in individual glasses.

SERVES 4

PREPARATION
35 minutes

STORAGE
You can refrigerate up to 3 days.

TRY THIS WITH...
party food—it's perfect for summer lunches.

HIGH IN...
antioxidants.

PROPERTIES
Cinnamon adds a dimension of blood-sugar balancing action, which makes it perfect for using in drinks as a substitute for sugar.

*sweet potato wedges

HIGH IN...
beta-carotene, fiber and vitamin A.

PROPERTIES
Sweet potatoes are a good alternative to white potatoes, because they release their sugars more slowly, helping to keep blood-sugar levels in balance.

These wedges are a nutrient-packed way to replace those less healthy potato chips. Sweet potato provides lots of vitamin A to protect your child's brain and it has also been classified as an anti-diabetic food because of its capacity to balance blood sugar so successfully. Roasting in olive oil is a much healthier alternative to frying, which can produce harmful free radicals; and the yogurt dip provides some beneficial bacteria.

2 large sweet potatoes, peeled and chopped into wedges
¼ cup olive oil
¼ teaspoon sea salt
1 teaspoon freshly ground black pepper
1 cup plain or Greek yogurt
2 tablespoons chopped cilantro
½ teaspoon celery salt

1 Heat the oven to 425°F. Place the sweet potato wedges in a medium baking dish.
2 Cover with the olive oil and season to taste with salt and pepper. Roast in the oven 30 to 40 minutes until the potatoes are soft.
3 Mix the cilantro and celery salt into the yogurt and serve in a small bowl as a dip for the sweet potato wedges.

SERVES 2

PREPARATION + COOKING
10 + 40 minutes

STORAGE
You can refrigerate for up to 2 days.

TRY THIS WITH...
hummus, salsa, or chive and sour cream dips – great in a lunchbox.

Some children will find plain yogurt with live cultures easier to tolerate than other yogurts.

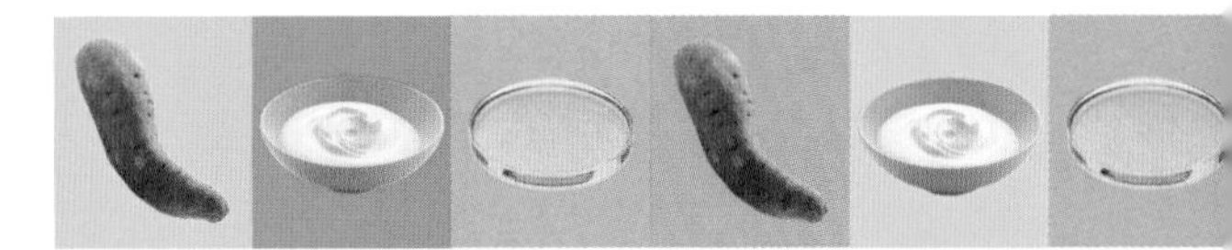

hummus rice snacks

SERVES 2

PREPARATION
5 minutes

STORAGE
Store in a dry place up to 4 hours.

TRY THIS WITH...
a vegetable salad and couscous for a light lunch.

HIGH IN...
B vitamins, fiber, monounsaturated fats, and vitamin C.

PROPERTIES
This topping has great anti-inflammatory and antioxidant properties—just like the famed beneficial Mediterranean diet that is its inspiration.

Rice cakes can be the perfect snack food, because they are so much higher in fiber than most other snacks. Your child, however, hould eat them with a source of protein, such as the hummus in this recipe, to slow down the quick release of sugars.

4 rice cakes
½ cup hummus
1 red bell pepper, seeded and sliced lengthwise
8 black olives, pitted and halved
4 sprigs basil

1 Spread each rice cake liberally with hummus and lay 3 or 4 strips of red pepper over each one.

2 Decorate with two olives and a sprig of basil and serve immediately.

V

veggie dippers

There really is no simpler way to eat vegetables than simply munching on them in their most natural form—raw. Getting your child used to snacking on raw vegetables like this can do wonders for his or her health, as none of the nutrients have been destroyed by cooking and the fiber is most intact. Even the necessary chewing is good for young teeth and gets the digestive juices flowing.

½ cup sour cream
1 handful chives, finely chopped
3 carrots, peeled and cut into strips
½ cup sugar snap peas
⅓ cup radishes
½ cucumber, cut into strips
½ red bell pepper, seeded and cut into strips
½ yellow bell pepper, seeded and cut into strips
6 sticks celery, cut into strips

1 In a small bowl, mix together the sour cream and chives.
2 Place the sour cream mixture in the middle of a large platter and arrange all the vegetable pieces around it, alternating the colors.

SERVES 2

PREPARATION
10 minutes

STORAGE
You can store the vegetables 24 hours if you keep them in cold water and refrigerate.

TRY THIS IN...
your child's lunchbox as an alternative to wheat-based sandwiches.

HIGH IN...
antioxidants, B vitamins, beta-carotene, fiber, potassium, and vitamins A, C, and E.

PROPERTIES
Raw vegetables are great for helping the body to detoxify and are particularly alkalizing for all the body systems: a good acid–alkaline balance helps the body to work as efficiently as possible.

celery smackers

Celery helps children to slow down as they eat because it requires a great deal of chewing, and it has a well-known calming effect on the whole nervous system. It contains apigenin, a substance which relaxes blood vessels and has been used for centuries as a traditional sleep remedy—what a perfect snack to whip out in those tense family moments!

SERVES 2

PREPARATION
5 minutes

STORAGE
You can refrigerate up to 24 hours.

TRY THIS WITH...
Creamed Salmon Rice Cakes (see page 39).

HIGH IN...
B vitamins, calcium, fiber, magnesium, and potassium.

PROPERTIES
The fiber in the celery, hummus, and cilantro helps remove toxins from the body, making this a thoroughly cleansing snack.

4 stalks celery, trimmed and cut into chunks
½ cup hummus
2 tablespoons chopped cilantro

1 Fill the groove in the celery chunks with the hummus, wiping away any excess.

2 Place the filled celery chunks on a plate and scatter the cilantro on top.

pecan pâté

Pecans are popular with children because of their creamy texture and sweet taste. They make an excellent basis for a nut pâté, and their strong flavor allows you to sneak in other beneficial ingredients, such as parsley and alfalfa, without your child noticing they are there.

1 cup shelled pecans
2 carrots, peeled and grated
½ cup alfalfa sprouts
1 tablespoon olive oil
½ teaspoon celery salt
4 tablespoons chopped parsley

1 Put the pecans into a blender and process until they have become crumblike. Add the carrots and alfalfa sprouts.

2 Process for another minute, then add the olive oil, celery salt, and parsley.

3 Blend the mixture together into a smooth pâté, adding extra olive oil, if necessary.

SERVES 2

PREPARATION
5 minutes

STORAGE
Refrigerate up to 5 days.

TRY THIS ON...
rice cakes or rye bread for a "good-mood" snack.

HIGH IN...
B vitamins, beta-carotene, fiber, omega-3 and -6 oils, magnesium, potassium, and zinc.

PROPERTIES
Pecans contain monounsaturated fats and omega-6 oils, both of which help to protect the body against the harm saturated fats can do.

cinnamon popcorn

HIGH IN...
fiber, folate, lysine, and vitamins B1 and B5.

PROPERTIES
Corn is high in the amino acid lysine, which helps to ward off viruses.

In the search for snacks that make both you and your child happy, this healthy version of an old favorite is a great find. Corn is a very high-fiber food, which means it helps to clear toxins from your child's body and stabilize fluctuating blood-sugar levels. Cinnamon is the perfect alternative to sugar: it has been shown to mimic the action of insulin, helping to move sugars from the corn (and other foods) out of the bloodstream and into cells, to help keep the body's blood sugars in balance.

2 tablespoons olive oil
⅓ cup popping corn
½ stick butter
1 teaspoon cinnamon

1 Heat the olive oil in a medium saucepan. Pour in the corn, put a lid on the pan, and shake it over the heat until the popping stops. Remove from the heat, leaving the lid on for a few minutes.
2 Melt the butter in a small, nonstick saucepan, then add the cinnamon and stir.
3 Pour the popcorn into a serving bowl and drizzle with the cinnamon butter.

SERVES 2

PREPARATION + COOKING
5 + 10 minutes

STORAGE
Store up to 3 days
in an airtight container.

TRY THIS AS...
a lunchbox filler and alternative
to chocolate bars or potato chips.

Organic popping corn contains fewer chemicals than regular popping corn.

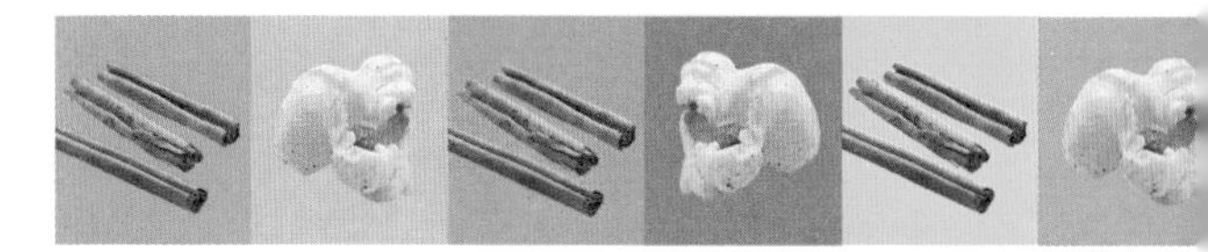

peanut butter cookies

MAKES 18

PREPARATION + COOKING
10 + 15 minutes

STORAGE
You can store the cookies up to a week in an airtight container; or freeze the unbaked dough up to 3 months.

TRY THIS WITH...
ice cream. Just break into pieces and sprinkle the cookies over vanilla ice cream.

HIGH IN...
B vitamins, fiber, potassium, protein, and tryptophan.

PROPERTIES
Peanuts are good sources of B vitamins (including folate and vitamin B3) and tryptophan, making this an excellent recipe for helping mood and brain function.

To make your cookies as healthy as possible use a wholenut variety of peanut butter from the health section of the supermarket or from a health-food store. When peanut butter is made from only ground whole peanuts it supplies lots of protein and fiber to really help reduce the sugar hit of the cookies.

1 stick butter, diced
½ cup packed light brown sugar
3 tablespoons wholenut peanut butter
1 banana
1¼ cups rye flour

1 Heat the oven to 375°F. Place the butter, sugar, and peanut butter in a small saucepan and heat gently to melt.
2 In a bowl, mash the banana with a fork and then add the flour and the melted peanut butter mixture. Stir together until the dough becomes sticky.
3 Form into walnut-size balls and press onto a greased cookie sheet leaving a good gap between each cookie. Bake in the oven 10 to 15 minutes until golden brown. Transfer to a wire rack to cool.

apricot & apple puree

Using fruits as sweet treats will help you to reach the high fruit-and-vegetable intake your child needs for optimum health. Making fruit purees is a great way to keep sweet treats, with no added sugar, around.

1 cup water
2 apples, peeled, cored, and cut into chunks
⅔ cup dried apricots
1 cup plain yogurt with live cultures

1 Pour the water into a small saucepan and add the apples and apricots.

2 Bring the water to a boil and then leave it to simmer 10 minutes, or until the fruit is soft. Remove from the heat and leave to cool 10 minutes, then pour into a blender and process until smooth. Refrigerate 30 to 40 minutes until chilled.

3 Spoon the yogurt into individual bowls and spoon equal amounts of the puree on top.

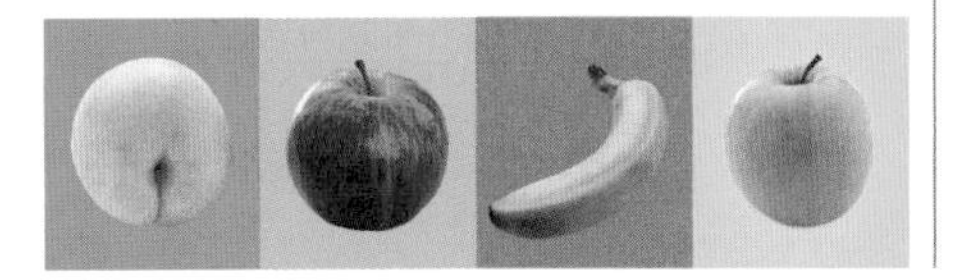

SERVES 4

PREPARATION + COOKING
5 + 10 minutes + chilling

STORAGE
You can keep the puree in the refrigerator up to 4 days.

TRY THIS AS...
a sauce for any dessert, or add seeds and yogurt to make a crunchy, creamy breakfast.

HIGH IN...
beta-carotene, fiber, manganese, and vitamins A, C, and K.

PROPERTIES
Apples contain a fiber called pectin that is particularly effective at carrying toxins out of the body and regulating bowel function.

soaked almonds

SERVES 4

PREPARATION
5 minutes + 12 hours soaking

STORAGE
Store the almonds in water 3 days, but replace the water frequently during that time.

TRY THIS AS...
delicious almond milk. Just put all the ingredients in a blender with some water and process until smooth.

HIGH IN...
B vitamins, calcium, fiber, magnesium, vitamin E, and zinc.

PROPERTIES
Almonds are high in zinc and vitamin E, both of which are important for skin health, helping to heal and prevent acne, eczema, psoriasis, and dermatitis.

Almonds are the perfect snack food as they are packed full with protein, fiber, vitamins, and minerals. They are also a wonderful antidote for sugar cravings because of their sweet taste. Soaking almonds in water helps to unlock their goodness.

1 cup whole almonds

½ cup dried almonds

1 Place the almonds in a large bowl and then fill the bowl with enough water to cover all the almonds.
2 Put the bowl in the refrigerator 12 hours. After the first six hours, drain the water and replace with fresh water.
3 After 12 hours, drain the water, add the dried almonds, and serve in a small snack bowl.

muesli crunchies

Somewhere between a bar cookie and muesli, these snack bars offer great taste and texture, so your children will love them. Nuts and seeds provide protein, and the oats insure a nice slow release of sugar to satisfy a sweet craving, without sending blood-sugar levels (and tempers) sky high.

1 stick butter
¼ cup packed light brown sugar
1 tablespoon blackstrap molasses
1½ cups rolled oats
⅓ cup pecans
½ cup sunflower seeds
⅓ cup golden raisins

1 Heat the oven to 400°F. Put the butter, sugar, and molasses into a saucepan and heat gently to melt.
2 In a bowl, stir together the remaining ingredients. Add the melted mixture and stir.
3 Press the dough into a shallow, nonstick baking pan, score into 2-inch squares and bake 20 minutes, or until golden brown. Cool in the pan for a few minutes, then cut along the score marks, and leave to cool on wire racks.

MAKES 12

PREPARATION + COOKING
10 + 20 minutes

STORAGE
Store the crunchies up to a week in an airtight container; or freeze the unbaked dough up to 3 months.

TRY THIS WITH...
plain yogurt for an on-the-go breakfast.

HIGH IN...
B vitamins, calcium, fiber, iron, magnesium, omega-6 oils, vitamin C, and zinc.

PROPERTIES
Molasses is the best sugar substitute as it contains many minerals, including iron, that are missing from sugar, as well as mood-enhancing properties.

DINNERS

Dinner need not be a struggle, even though it comes at the time of the day when everyone in the family is tired. Here are some simple supper options that provide a relaxing end to the day and help your child wind down. To ease this process, encourage your child to eat at least an hour before bedtime to allow time for full digestion before sleep. Although we tend to think of dinner as our main meal of the day, it often suits children (and for that matter adults) better to have a substantial lunch and lighter evening meal. If lunch has been a snack, however, a child's dinner should include all the essential nutrients that will insure he or she maintains a healthy diet.

mushroom omelets

An omelet is always a good way to hold together ingredients and introduce your child to new foods. This recipe provides all of the building blocks for healthy brain function and promotes regular sleep patterns.

MAKES 2

PREPARATION + COOKING
5 + 15 minutes

STORAGE
Eat omelets immediately after cooking.

TRY THIS WITH...
Crunchy Country Salad (see page 92).

HIGH IN...
B vitamins, calcium, magnesium, tryptophan, and vitamin K.

PROPERTIES
Goat cheese can be a healthy alternative to cow's-milk cheese, as it is easier to digest and contains lots of tryptophan, which helps to manufacture the happy hormone serotonin.

5 eggs
½ teaspoon freshly ground black pepper
¼ teaspoon celery salt
1 teaspoon dried oregano
5 tablespoons milk
1 tablespoon olive oil
1 red onion, diced
1⅔ cups sliced mushrooms
½ cup goat cheese
2 tablespoons chopped parsley

1 Put the eggs into a small bowl and beat with a fork. Add the pepper, salt, oregano, and milk, stirring together well.
2 Heat half the oil in a small skillet. Add the onion and mushrooms and sauté until soft.
3 Remove the pan from the heat and drain off any excess oil. Add the onion and mushrooms to the beaten eggs and stir. Heat the remaining oil in the skillet. Add half the mixture and cook the omelet 3 to 4 minutes.
4 Crumble half the goat cheese on top, then flip the omelet and cook the other side. Repeat with the remaining ingredients to make the second omlet. Serve on individual plates, sprinkled with parsley.

potato skin battalions

Keeping potatoes in their skins retains a whole set of nutrients that are lost when you use just the starchy inner part. The skin also acts as the perfect little bowl, making these battalions fun to pick up and eat with fingers.

3 medium potatoes, baked
8 scallions, chopped
⅓ cup plain yogurt with live cultures
½ cup tomato salsa
6 sprigs cilantro

1 Heat the oven to 350°F. Bake the potatoes in the oven 1 hour. Alternatively, you can cook them in a microwave 10 minutes, or until soft.

2 Halve the potatoes. Scoop the soft potato out of the skins and into a bowl. Mix in the onion and yogurt, mashing together with a fork.

3 Put the mixture back into the potato skins, garnish with a dollop of salsa and a sprig of cilantro and serve.

SERVES 3

PREPARATION + COOKING
15 minutes + 1 hour

STORAGE
You can refrigerate up to 2 or 3 days.

TRY THIS WITH...
Crunchy Country Salad (see page 92), steamed asparagus, or in a lunchbox.

HIGH IN...
beneficial bacteria, fiber, potassium, and vitamin C.

PROPERTIES
The skin of the potato contains the best fiber, which helps to keep the digestive system healthy. Most of the immune-boosting vitamin C is found just below the skin.

sweet potato patties

MAKES 12 TO 15 PATTIES

PREPARATION + COOKING
10 + 25 minutes

STORAGE
You can refrigerate the raw mixture and use within 3 days, or freeze it up to a month.

TRY THIS WITH...
some sweet onion pickle or a sour cream and chive dip.

HIGH IN...
B vitamins, beta-carotene, fiber, magnesium, and vitamin A.

PROPERTIES
Cilantro, grown from coriander seed, has a reputation as an anti-diabetic herb owing to its ability to balance blood sugar; it is also full of substances that help to bring down inflammation.

These are fantastic finger-foods and snacks. The sweet potato can satisfy a child's demand for something sweet, while actually helping to regulate blood-sugar levels and calm down your child's nervous system. Keep a batch in the freezer for when you need something calming in the evening.

2 large sweet potatoes, peeled and chopped
1 cup canned chickpeas, drained
1 tablespoon olive oil
1 teaspoon coriander seeds
2 teaspoons Dijon mustard
½ tablespoon olive oil

1 Half fill a saucepan with water and bring to a boil. Add the sweet potatoes, cover, and leave to simmer 15 to 20 minutes until soft.

2 Drain the sweet potatoes and put into a mixing bowl. Add the chickpeas, olive oil, coriander seeds, and Dijon mustard. Using a potato masher, mash together. Use your hands to mold the mixture into 12 to 15 balls.

3 Heat the olive oil in a nonstick skillet. Add the potato balls, one at a time. Use a spatula to press into a patty shape. Turn over and cook until light brown on both sides, then serve.

towering turkey bagels

Turkey is the meat lowest in saturated fat, and it's very high in tryptophan—which is probably why we tend to fall asleep after Thanksgiving dinner! This recipe is simple to make, filling, and will send your child into a deep sleep.

1 4-ounce piece skinless turkey breast meat
2 sesame or wholewheat bagels
2 tablespoons cranberry sauce
2 tablespoons mayonnaise
2 handfuls arugula
2 sprigs cilantro
2 scallions

1 Heat the broiler to high. Place the turkey on a broiler pan and broil 10 minutes, turning occasionally. Remove from the heat, cool, and slice thinly. Cut the bagels in half horizontally and toast lightly.

2 Spread one half of each bagel with the cranberry sauce. Place the turkey on top and cover with a handful of arugula and a sprig of cilantro. Spread mayonnaise on the other two halves.

3 Cut the scallions into four pieces, then again in half lengthwise. Lay these on top of the arugula. Put the two bagel slices together, cut in half, and serve.

SERVES 2

PREPARATION + COOKING
10 + 10 minutes

STORAGE
Refrigerate up to 1 day.

TRY THIS WITH...
Sweet Potato Wedges (see pages 72–3).

HIGH IN...
protein, selenium, tryptophan, and vitamins B3 and B6.

PROPERTIES
Turkey is a great source of the mineral selenium, which is crucial for liver function and for producing your child's body's antioxidant enzymes.

tuna melts

SERVES 2

PREPARATION + COOKING
10 + 5 minutes

STORAGE
Refrigerate and eat cold later the same day if you wish.

TRY THIS WITH...
Roast Peppers (see page 110).

HIGH IN...
B vitamins, manganese, protein, vitamin K, and zinc.

PROPERTIES
Wholewheat pitas provide a lot more nutrients than their white counterparts; for example, about 70 percent of magnesium is lost in refining flour to make it white.

An easy and comforting meal for the end of a busy day, these delicious tuna melts belie a host of protein and nutrients, including the mineral manganese, which helps to balance blood sugar, crucial for deep and undisturbed sleep during the night.

4 wholewheat pita breads
2 cans (6-oz) tuna in olive oil, drained
6 scallions, chopped
½ teaspoon cayenne pepper
2 tablespoons chopped parsley
4 ounces goat cheese

1 Heat the broiler to medium. Cut the pitas in half, then place under the broiler 1 minute, or until lightly toasted.
2 In a mixing bowl, combine the tuna, scallions, cayenne pepper, and parsley. Mix together well with a fork and then spoon the tuna mixture equally into each pita.
3 Crumble the goat cheese into the bowl, mix, and then fill each pita with an equal amount. Place the pitas on the broiler pan and broil until the cheese melts. Serve hot.

sardine soldiers

Although it is always best to present your children with fresh fish, sometimes we need simple convenience, and some canned foods provide a quick, healthy solution straight from the cupboard. Sardines are a great source of omega-3 oils, the levels of which are hardly affected by the canning process.

4 slices wholegrain bread
1 can (2-oz) sardines in tomato sauce
2 tablespoons chopped parsley
4 sprigs parsley

1 Heat the broiler to medium. Lightly toast the bread, then butter one side and cut each slice into two triangles.
2 In a small bowl, combine the sardines and parsley and mash together with a fork. Spread the sardine mixture equally onto the pieces of toast.
3 Return the toast to the broiler pan and broil 5 minutes, or until the tops brown. Serve on individual plates, garnished with the parsley sprigs.

SERVES 2

PREPARATION + COOKING
5 + 5 minutes

STORAGE
Refrigerate up to 12 hours in airtight container.

TRY THIS AS...
a lunchtime snack, or served with a light salad.

HIGH IN...
B vitamins, calcium, iron, lycopene, omega-3 oils, potassium, vitamin K, and zinc.

PROPERTIES
The protein in fish is excellent quality and easy for your child to absorb, as it is highly digestible and supports gut health.

crunchy country salad

Beets are colorful, attractive, and sweet—and also extremely healthy, as they are packed full of antioxidants.

SERVES 2

PREPARATION + COOKING
10 + 5 minutes

STORAGE
Store in the refrigerator 1 day only.

TRY THIS WITH...
Mushroom & Spinach Quiche (see page 111) or Roast Peppers (see page 110).

HIGH IN...
anthocyanidin, beta-cyanin, antioxidants, B vitamins, fiber, folate, omega-6 oils, and potassium.

PROPERTIES
The beta-cyanin in beets gives them their deep purple color and is a highly effective detoxifying agent.

⅔ cup shelled lima beans
1⅓ cups arugula
½ red onion, sliced
1 cooked beet, grated
2 stalks celery, grated
4 plum tomatoes, sliced
2 tablespoons sunflower seeds
4 tablespoons olive oil
1 teaspoon horseradish sauce (make sure it's wheat- and gluten-free)
1 teaspoon honey
1 teaspoon dried oregano

1 Half fill a small saucepan with water and bring to a boil. Add the lima beans, cover, and leave to simmer 5 minutes, or until cooked. Remove the pan from the heat, drain, and leave to cool completely.

2 Place the arugula in a large salad bowl, then add the onion, beet, celery, tomatoes, and the cool lima beans. Scatter the sunflower seeds on top.

3 In a bowl, mix together the olive oil, horseradish, honey, and oregano. Drizzle over the salad and serve.

bright bean salad

Bright colors will help sell a dish to your child and this one is virtually technicolored! It's also a meeting of superfoods, and a fine addition to your weekly menu for all aspects of your child's health and happiness.

3 tablespoons olive oil
2 zucchini, sliced thinly
leaves of 2 hearts of lettuces
½ cup alfalfa sprouts
2 small beets, grated
1 can (15-oz) mixed beans, drained
1 avocado, peeled and sliced
4 ounces cherry tomatoes, cut in half
1 teaspoon dried oregano
2 tablespoons balsamic vinegar
2 tablespoons chopped parsley

1 Heat a large wok with 1 tablespoon of the oil. Sauté the zucchini until golden brown, then remove from the heat.

2 Arrange the lettuce leaves in a serving bowl and add the sprouts, beets, beans, and avocado. Scatter the tomatoes and zucchini on top.

3 Sprinkle the oregano, balsamic vinegar, and remaining olive oil over the salad. Garnish with the parsley and serve.

SERVES 4

PREPARATION + COOKING
10 + 5 minutes

STORAGE
Eat the salad fresh, immediately after it is made.

TRY THIS WITH...
Sweet Potato Scorchers (see page 88).

HIGH IN...
antioxidants, B vitamins, beneficial (monounsaturated) fats, fiber, magnesium, and zinc.

PROPERTIES
Avocados are remarkably high in fiber and a great source of healthy monounsaturated fats, which have anti-inflammatory properties, and promote good circulation and heart health.

smiley face pizza

HIGH IN...
lutein, lycopene, protein, and vitamin C.

PROPERTIES
The full range of colors on this pizza represents the variety of plant chemicals it provides—all of which protect your child's immune system.

Tomatoes, onions, and peppers provide a host of antioxidants, including vitamin C, vitamin A and carotenoids, which protect the developing brain. The pizza is also a good source of vitamin B6 and folate, which are vital to regulate mood throughout the day.

2 cheese and tomato pizza crusts
½ small red onion, peeled
3½ ounces goat cheese
3 ounces cooked ham, sliced
½ red bell pepper, seeded and thinly sliced
½ yellow bell pepper, seeded and thinly sliced
2 olives, stuffed with pimiento
1 teaspoon oregano
a small handful arugula
10 cherry tomatoes, halved
balsamic vinegar

1 Heat the oven to 425°F. Place the pizza crusts on a nonstick baking sheet.

2 Slice the red onion into rings. Remove the inner rings and place on the pizza base as eyes. Cut two slices from the goat cheese and place beneath the onions as a nose.

3 Place a ham slice on the pizza in a curved line and top with a pepper strip to create a smile. Alternate the colored pepper strips for hair. Halve the stuffed olives and put these in the middle of the onion rings as pupils.

4 Sprinkle the pizzas with oregano, then bake in the oven 15 minutes.

5 Put the arugula and tomatoes in a salad bowl, drizzle with balsamic vinegar, and serve with the pizzas.

SERVES 2

PREPARATION + COOKING
10 + 15 minutes

STORAGE
You can refrigerate up to 3 days.

TRY THIS WITH...
tuna if you need a more filling meal. This will keep energy levels high but stable.

If your child is sensitive to goat cheese, omit it from the recipe and use an extra slice of tomato for the nose.

pan-fried turkey

SERVES 2

PREPARATION + COOKING
5 + 10 minutes

STORAGE
Eat this dish immediately after cooking.

TRY THIS WITH...
Minted Potatoes with Hazelnuts (see page 116).

HIGH IN...
B vitamins, fiber, magnesium, protein, tryptophan, and vitamins A and K.

PROPERTIES
Green beans are a great way for kids to obtain high levels of vitamins A and K, which are essential for bone-building.

This delicious, calm-inducing meal takes virtually no time to prepare. With its high levels of brain-boosting nutrients, this meal helps kids to recover after a busy day, and they will love the sweetness of the cranberries and the crunch of the beans.

½ stick butter
2 turkey breasts halves, about 5 ounces each
4 ounces green beans
½ tablespoon olive oil
4 scallions, chopped
2 garlic cloves, thinly sliced
juice of 1 lime
4 tablespoons cranberry sauce
2 tablespoons chopped parsley

1 Melt the butter in a skillet. Add the turkey breasts and slowly cook until light brown on each side.
2 Meanwhile, half fill a saucepan with water and bring to a boil. Add the green beans and simmer 5 minutes.
3 In a separate saucepan, heat the olive oil and sauté the scallions and garlic 30 seconds. Add the lime juice and cranberry sauce and stir over low heat 2 minutes.
4 Place the turkey breasts on individual plates, pour the cranberry and lime sauce on top, garnish with the chopped parsley, and serve with the beans on the side.

chicken & coconut curry

Curry might seem too spicy for children, but they will adore this sweet, mild version.

1½ cups brown rice
2 tablespoons butter
3 skinless chicken breast halves, about 6 ounces each, sliced
2 small onions, sliced
2 garlic cloves, crushed
1 tablespoon coriander seeds
½ cup cashew nuts
⅓ cup raisins
2 tablespoons lime pickle
3 cups shredded spinach
½ teaspoon cayenne pepper
2 cups water
1 tablespoon vegetable bouillon powder
2 tablespoons mango chutney
1 cup coconut milk

1 Half fill a saucepan with water and bring to a boil. Add the rice, cover, and simmer 15 to 20 minutes until soft.
2 Meanwhile, melt the butter in a saucepan. Add the chicken and brown over low heat. Add the onions and garlic and sauté until soft.
3 Add the seeds, nuts, raisins, pickle, spinach, cayenne pepper, water, and bouillon powder and simmer 15 minutes, stirring occasionally. Add the remaining ingredients and simmer 3 to 5 minutes longer. Remove the rice from the heat and drain. Serve on individual plates with the curry divided equally on top.

SERVES 4

PREPARATION + COOKING
10 + 40 minutes

STORAGE
You can refrigerate the curry 2 to 3 days, or freeze it for up to a month.

TRY THIS AS...
a soup, blending the curry sauce in a food processor, or serve with brown basmati rice.

HIGH IN...
beneficial fats (MCTs—medium-chain triglycerides—which the body uses as energy), fiber, folate, magnesium, protein, and tryptophan.

PROPERTIES
coconut contains a substance called lauric acid, which is highly protective against disease and infection.

honey links & mashed potatoes

Choose good-quality sausages, following the guidelines on page 54. Combined with the protein in the sausages, the sugars in mashed potatoes enter the bloodstream slowly.

SERVES 4

PREPARATION + COOKING
10 + 20 minutes

STORAGE
Once cooked, you can refrigerate the sausages to eat within 24 hours.

TRY THIS WITH...
cocktail sausages for a party treat.

HIGH IN...
folate, magnesium, potassium, protein, and selenium.

PROPERTIES
Mustard seeds are a close relative of broccoli and cabbage and have similar liver-supporting properties, helping to rid your child's body of harmful toxins.

1 pound 2 ounces Idaho potatoes, peeled and cut into chunks
4 tablespoons honey
6 tablespoons wholegrain mustard
8 link sausages
1 cup shelled peas
⅓ cup milk
1 tablespoon butter

1 Heat the oven to 375°F. Half fill a saucepan with water and bring to a boil. Add the potatoes, cover, and simmer 15 to 20 minutes, until soft.

2 Meanwhile, mix the honey and mustard in a small bowl. Prick the sausages with a fork and place in a baking dish. Pour the mustard and honey sauce over and bake 20 minutes until brown.

3 Half fill another saucepan with water and bring to a boil. Add the peas, cover, and simmer 5 minutes until cooked. Add the milk and butter to the potatoes and mash. Remove the sausages from the oven, drain the peas, and serve with the mashed potatoes on individual plates.

mamma's meatballs

These meatballs are made with lean ground meat, and seeds, eggs, and herbs, making them both nutritious and delicious!

1 tablespoon olive oil
1 onion, diced
1 leek, trimmed and sliced
2 garlic cloves, thinly sliced
4 slices wholewheat bread, crusts removed
1 teaspoon dried oregano
1 pound 2 ounces ground lamb
55g/2oz/⅓ cup sunflower seeds
2 tablespoons chopped cilantro
2 tablespoons chopped parsley
1 tablespoon wholegrain mustard
2 eggs
2 cups brown rice
½ teaspoon cinnamon
1 cup jarred tomato sauce
scant ½ cup tomato paste
1 tablespoon Worcestershire sauce

1 Heat the oven to 375°F. In a wok, heat the oil and stir-fry the onion, leek, and garlic until soft.
2 Whiz the bread in a food processor to make crumbs, then transfer the crumbs to a mixing bowl and mix in the oregano, lamb, seeds, herbs, mustard, and eggs. Using your hands, mold the mixture into small meatballs. Place on a baking tray and bake 20 to 30 minutes. Meanwhile, add the rice to boiling water and simmer 20 minutes.
3 Put the tomato sauce, paste, and Worcestershire sauce into a separate small pan and stir over low heat. Serve the sauce over the rice and meatballs.

SERVES 4

PREPARATION + COOKING
10 + 30 minutes

STORAGE
You can refrigerate the raw mixture up to 3 days.

TRY THIS WITH...
baked or mashed potatoes instead of rice. These are a great alternative to burgers.

HIGH IN...
protein, selenium, tryptophan, vitamins B3 and B12, and zinc.

PROPERTIES
Lamb is high in tryptophan and is therefore a great dinner choice as it prepares the body to make serotonin for a good night's sleep.

orange-roasted lamb chops

SERVES 4

PREPARATION + COOKING
5 + 30 minutes

STORAGE
Prepare the chops in advance and store them uncooked in the refrigerator up to 12 hours.

TRY THIS WITH...
green beans, mashed potatoes, and red currant jelly.

HIGH IN...
antioxidants, B vitamins, protein, tryptophan, and vitamin C.

PROPERTIES
Cloves are highly effective at killing off bacteria and viruses, and help to calm down any digestive upsets.

Cooking lamb with orange juice helps to break down the meat to make it more easily digestible, and easier for children to absorb its protein, iron, and vitamin B12. Antioxidant foods, such as oranges and rosemary, help to protect against harmful free radicals that can be produced during cooking.

2 teaspoons butter
8 lamb chops, about 2 ounces each
4 cloves
2 oranges, the grated peel of 1 and juice of both
8 sprigs rosemary
2 tablespoons chopped mint

1 Heat the oven to 400°F. Spread the butter over the lamb chops on both sides and lay them in a shallow baking dish.
2 Add the cloves, orange zest, juice, and rosemary. Place in the oven 30 minutes, turning the chops once during cooking.
3 Remove the dish from the oven and serve the chops on individual plates, garnished with the chopped mint.

baked cod with salsa

Cod is a great source of protein, but it doesn't have the saturated-fat content of meat. It is also good for soaking up other flavors, such as this salsa, which is high in compounds that both support immunity and aid digestion.

1 small yellow bell pepper, seeded and finely diced
3 plum tomatoes, finely diced
½ red onion, finely diced
¼ cucumber, finely diced
1½ tablespoons olive oil
1 tablespoon chopped cilantro
2 cod fillets, about 5 ounces each
½ lemon, sliced

1 Heat the oven to 400°F. Place all the vegetables in a bowl and add the olive oil and cilantro.
2 Put the fish fillets in a small baking dish and pour the salsa mix over the top.
3 Cover the dish with foil and bake 15 minutes, or until the fish is cooked. Serve garnished with the lemon slices.

SERVES 2

PREPARATION + COOKING
10 + 15 minutes

STORAGE
You can prepare this dish in advance and refrigerate up to 6 hours before cooking.

TRY THIS WITH...
a green salad or some lightly stir-fried snow peas with sesame seeds.

HIGH IN...
B vitamins, protein, tryptophan, and vitamin D.

PROPERTIES
Cod is a fantastic source of tryptophan and also has high levels of vitamins B3, B6, and B12—altogether a great combination for focus, good mood, and healthy sleep patterns.

tuna steak kabobs & sugar snaps

SERVES 2

PREPARATION + COOKING
10 + 10 minutes

STORAGE
Keep the kabobs uncooked in the refrigerator no longer than 12 hours.

TRY THIS WITH...
stir-fried noodles with soy sauce.

HIGH IN...
B vitamins, lycopene, omega-3 and -6 oils, protein, and zinc.

PROPERTIES
Sesame seeds contain a unique compound called sesamin that helps protect the heart and liver and also helps to carry the antioxidant vitamin E into the body.

This is a hearty alternative to a meat dish, as tuna steaks have a similar texture to meat, but are packed with essential omega-3 oils rather than saturated fats. The inclusion of sesame oil and seeds provides omega-6 oils for balance, as well as an appealing nutty taste.

2 tuna steaks, cut into ¾-inch cubes
16 cherry tomatoes
1 tablespoon bottled pesto sauce
1 tablespoon sesame oil
7 ounces sugar snap peas
1 tablespoon sesame seeds

1 Heat the broiler to high. Load two kabob skewers with the tuna cubes and cherry tomatoes. Baste the kabobs with the pesto and place under the broiler 10 minutes, turning occasionally, until cooked through.
2 Heat the sesame oil in a wok. Add the sugar snap peas and stir-fry about 4 minutes. Add the sesame seeds, stir, and remove from the heat.
3 Divide the sugar snaps between two plates. Remove the kabobs from the heat and place on top of the peas.

salmon with mango salsa

All the ingredients in this recipe are superstars in the immunity stakes, as they cover the full range of antioxidants.

4 salmon fillets, about 5 ounces each, skinned
1 tablespoon olive oil
2 garlic cloves, thinly sliced
6 scallions, chopped
1 mango, peeled, seeded, and diced into small pieces
juice of 2 limes
1 teaspoon chopped gingerroot
½ teaspoon chili powder
3 tablespoons mango chutney

1 Heat the broiler to medium. Place the salmon on a broiler pan and broil 5 to 6 minutes on each side.

2 Meanwhile, heat the olive oil in a small saucepan. Add the garlic and scallions and sauté 30 seconds. Add the diced mango, lime juice, ginger, and chili powder and stir over low heat 1 minute. Stir in the mango chutney and remove from the heat. Put the salmon onto plates and spoon the salsa equally on top of each fillet.

SERVES 4

PREPARATION + COOKING
10 + 6 minutes

STORAGE
The salsa will keep in the refrigerator up to 3 days.

TRY THIS WITH...
Sesame Asian Greens (see page 118).

HIGH IN...
B vitamins, beta-carotene, omega-3 oils, potassium, vitamins A and C, and zinc.

PROPERTIES
The beautiful orange color of mango comes from its high levels of beta-carotene, which, together with the omega-3 oils in the salmon, protect the skin and support immunity.

pumpkin soup

SERVES 2

PREPARATION + COOKING
5 + 20 minutes

STORAGE
You can refrigerate up to 3 days or freeze up to a month.

TRY THIS AS...
a steamy soup in a flask for a child's lunchbox on a cold day.

HIGH IN...
beta-carotene, potassium, and vitamins A and C.

PROPERTIES
The vibrant orange color of pumpkin comes from its high levels of beta-carotene, which our bodies can convert to vitamin A to boost skin and eye health.

Pumpkin is a beautiful, rich-colored and subtle-tasting vine fruit many children think of as a jack-o'-lantern rather than something they can eat. Choose small pumpkins for the tastiest, juiciest flesh.

1 tablespoon olive oil
1 onion, diced
1 14-ounce pumpkin, peeled and seeded
2½ cups water
4 teaspoons vegetable bouillon powder
1 teaspoon grated nutmeg
½ teaspoon cinnamon
½ teaspoon freshly ground black pepper

1 Heat the oil in a large saucepan. Add the onion and pumpkin and sauté 4 minutes, stirring occasionally. Add the water, bouillon powder, nutmeg, and cinnamon.

2 Cover and simmer 10 to 15 minutes until the pumpkin is soft. Remove from the heat and let cool 10 minutes.

3 Pour into a blender and process until smooth. Serve in individual bowls and garnish with the ground black pepper.

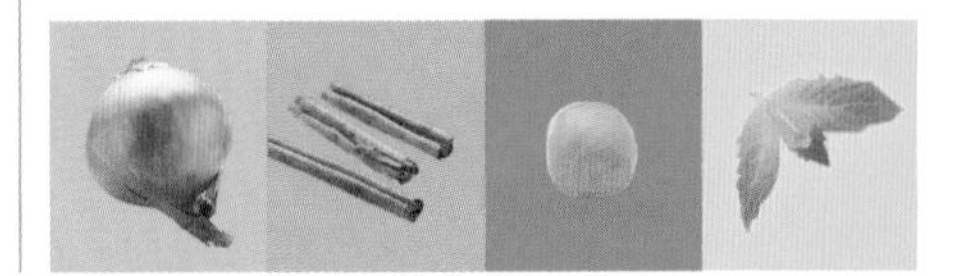

V

pea & mint soup with panini

Peas are the ultimate convenience food, as you can keep them in the freezer, and they retain their nutrient levels extremely well during the freezing process. Soups are a great way to get nutrients into your child in a form that is easy for the body to absorb.

2 tablespoons butter
6 scallions, chopped
2½ cups water
2 cups shelled peas
2 tablespoons chopped mint leaves
4 tablespoons vegetable bouillon powder
2 panini or Italian bread
2 sprigs mint

1 Melt the butter in a medium saucepan over low heat. Add the scallions, sauté 30 seconds, then add the water, peas, mint, and bouillon powder. Leave to simmer 10 minutes.
2 Meanwhile, cut the panini or Italian bread in half and toast lightly. Set aside.
3 Pour the soup into a blender and process until smooth. Pour into individual bowls, garnish each with a sprig of mint, and serve with the toasted panini or bread.

SERVES 2

PREPARATION + COOKING
5 + 20 minutes

STORAGE
You can refrigerate up to 3 days or freeze up to a month.

TRY THIS WITH...
a scoop of sour cream and chopped chives.

HIGH IN...
fiber, folate, manganese, and vitamins A, C, and K.

PROPERTIES
Peas are an excellent mood food with high levels of folate, which is crucial for growth, neural development, and to help prevent depression.

SERVES 4

PREPARATION + COOKING
10 + 20 minutes

STORAGE
Freeze this up to a month or refrigerate leftovers and use within 2 days.

TRY THIS WITH...
other green leafy vegetables, such as watercress or curly kale, or beans.

HIGH IN...
B vitamins, calcium, fiber, magnesium, sulfur, and vitamin C.

PROPERTIES
Like its cousin broccoli, cabbage has great detoxifying properties and is also very high in vitamin C for immune support.

V

spring greens broth

Cabbage does not have to be a dull, limp, tasteless affair, reminiscent of overcooked school lunches. Cooked properly, cabbage is both flavorsome and healthy, bursting with many of the vitamins and minerals that are essential for your child's development.

1 tablespoon olive oil
8 scallions, chopped
1 onion, sliced
2 garlic cloves, crushed
2 cups shredded green cabbage
3 cups chopped spinach
⅓ cup sunflower seeds
4 teaspoons bottled pesto sauce
3⅓ cups water
4 teaspoons vegetable bouillon powder
2 tablespoons chopped parsley

1 Heat the oil in a saucepan. Add the onions and garlic and sau 2 minutes. Add the remaining ingredients, except the parsl cover, and simmer 15 minutes.

2 Remove from the heat. Place the soup in a blender and proce until smooth. Pour into individual bowls, sprinkle wi parsley, and serve.

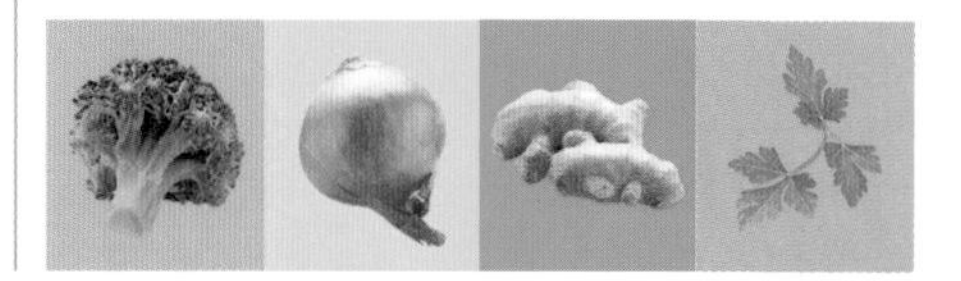

071

broccoli & ginger stir-fry

Stir-fries are among the best and easiest ways to cook vegetables, as the vegetables retain their fiber and other nutrient levels. Use stir-fries as opportunities to introduce small amounts of new foods to your child to expand their dietary repertoire.

4 tablespoons sesame oil
1½ cups chopped broccoli
1¾ cups shredded curly kale
1 garlic clove, chopped
2 teaspoons chopped gingerroot
6 scallions, sliced
3 tablespoons tamari soy sauce
5 ounces udon noodles (check they are gluten-free)
2 tablespoons sesame seeds
1 tablespoon chopped cilantro

1 Heat the sesame oil in a wok. Add the broccoli and curly kale and stir-fry 3 to 5 minutes. Add the garlic, ginger, scallions, and soy sauce and continue to stir.

2 Add the udon noodles, sesame seeds, and, if required, a little more soy sauce. Keep stirring over high heat 3 to 5 minutes longer until the vegetables are cooked lightly and still crunchy.

3 Remove from the heat and serve on individual plates, garnished with the cilantro.

SERVES 2

PREPARATION + COOKING
5 + 12 minutes

STORAGE
This meal can be delicious cold and will retain its freshness up to 2 days if refrigerated.

TRY THIS WITH...
two chicken breast halves for a meat alternative.

HIGH IN...
antioxidants, B vitamins, calcium, fiber, magnesium, and sulfur.

PROPERTIES
The combination of broccoli and ginger provides one of the best insurance policies against poor health for your child—they are quite literally packed with antioxidants.

pesto, spinach & mushroom tagliatelle

Pesto is a really useful ingredient to keep in the refrigerator if you want to some zing to a variety of meals. It goes well with spinach, and includes antibacterial and antiviral garlic, which helps ward off those playground bugs.

SERVES 2

PREPARATION + COOKING
5 + 20 minutes

STORAGE
Keep the sauce refrigerated 2 to 3 days, but use fresh pasta.

TRY THIS WITH...
a green salad on the side, or serve with mixed-grain bread and olive oil.

HIGH IN...
folate, iron, magnesium, manganese, and vitamins A, C, and K.

PROPERTIES
Spinach is a true superfood: it is packed with nutrients, but also high in protein, and it is a good anti-inflammatory food, shown to prevent some major diseases.

6 ounces fresh spinach tagliatelle
4 tablespoons olive oil
1 onion, diced
1 garlic clove, thinly sliced
⅓ cup pine nuts
2 cups chopped spinach
1½ cups sliced mushrooms
3 tablespoons bottled arugula pesto sauce
⅔ cup grated Parmesan cheese

1 Half fill a saucepan with water and bring to a boil. Add the tagliatelle and 1 tablespoon olive oil, cover, and cook until al dente (see package for cooking times).
2 Meanwhile, heat the rest of the olive oil in a saucepan. Add the onion, garlic, and pine nuts and sauté 1 minute. Add the spinach and mushrooms and simmer 5 minutes. Add the pesto, stir 1 minute, and remove from the heat.
3 Drain the pasta and divide onto individual plates. Spoon the sauce equally over the pasta and sprinkle with the grated Parmesan.

polenta & pepper cakes with pesto

Polenta, a Italian form of cornmeal, is a useful base ingredient for snacks and salads.

2 tablespoons olive oil
1 red bell pepper, seeded and diced
heaped ¾ cup baby zucchini, sliced
1 red onion, diced
¾ cup chopped broccoli
2 garlic cloves, thinly sliced
1⅔ cups sliced mushrooms
1½ quarts water
2¼ cups polenta
½ cup grated cheddar cheese
2 tablespoons bottled pesto sauce
6 sprigs fresh basil

1 Heat the oven to 350°F. and heat the oil in a skillet. Add the vegetables and garlic and sauté 5 to 6 minutes until light brown.

2 Meanwhile, in a saucepan, bring the water to a boil. Add the polenta and simmer, stirring, 15 to 20 minutes until it leaves the sides of the pan and thickens. Remove from the heat and mix in the cheese and vegetables.

3 Mold the mixture into cakes, place on a nonstick baking sheet, and put in the oven 20 minutes, or until light brown. Serve on individual plates with a little pesto drizzled over each cake. Garnish with basil sprigs.

SERVES 2

PREPARATION + COOKING
10 + 20 minutes

STORAGE
You can refrigerate the uncooked polenta up to 2 days or freeze it up to a month.

TRY THIS WITH...
Steamy Soup
(see page 43).

HIGH IN...
B vitamins, lysine, magnesium, selenium, sulfur, and vitamin C.

PROPERTIES
Corn has high levels of an amino acid called lysine, which is particularly effective at killing off viruses.

stuffed roast peppers

You can buy bell peppers in various colors, but the yellow variety has a sweeter, milder flavor than its red, green, or orange cousins. Stuffing vegetables is a great way to present new foods to your child—chopped and concealed within!

SERVES 6

PREPARATION + COOKING
10 + 30 minutes

STORAGE
Keep the stuffed peppers in the refrigerator up to 2 days.

TRY THIS WITH...
Crunchy Country Salad (see page 92).

HIGH IN...
beta-carotene, beneficial oils, fiber, folate, and vitamins A and C.

PROPERTIES
Bell peppers are known to help digestion by stimulating the production of digestive juices. These help your child to absorb the highest possible levels of nutrients from the meal.

6 yellow bell peppers
½ cup water
⅓ cup couscous
1 tablespoon olive oil
1 red onion, diced
2 garlic cloves, thinly sliced
1⅔ cups chopped asparagus
2 cups chopped spinach
⅓ cup pine nuts
⅓ cup crumbled feta cheese
1 teaspoon dried oregano
2 tablespoons chopped parsley

1 Heat the oven to 400°F. Cut the tops off the peppers, core them, remove the seeds, and set aside. Pour the water into a saucepan and bring to a boil. Add the couscous and leave to simmer until the water is absorbed, about 10 minutes. Remove from the heat.

2 In a wok, heat the olive oil. Add the onion, garlic, asparagus, spinach, and pine nuts, and stir-fry 1 to 2 minutes, or until the asparagus is soft. Remove from the heat, add the feta, oregano, and couscous, mixing well. Spoon into the peppers and place in a shallow baking dish.

3 Drizzle with olive oil and bake 10 to 15 minutes until light brown. Serve garnished with the chopped parsley.

mushroom & spinach quiche

Quiche can provide a wholesome and hearty meal. You can buy ready-to-roll pastry, but making your own enables you to use healthier rye rather than wheat flour.

2 cups light rye flour
3 tablespoons ground almonds
9 tablespoonsbutter
3 tablespoons water
2 cups chopped spinach
1 onion, chopped
1⅔ cups sliced mushrooms
2 whole eggs
2 egg yolks
1 cup light cream
1 pinch celery salt
⅔ cup goat cheese

1 Heat the oven to 400°F.

2 Put the flour and ground almonds, and 8 tablespoons (1 stick) of the butter into a bowl. Mix in the butter with your fingers until it is like bread crumbs. Add the water and knead together. Roll out on a countertop into a large circle and place in a greased 8-inch quiche pan.

3 Melt the remaining butter in a wok. Add the spinach, onion, and mushrooms and stir-fry 5 minutes until brown.

4 Whisk together the eggs, yolks, cream, and celery salt. Pour the vegetables into the pan, sprinkle the goat cheese on top and pour the egg mixture over. Bake 20 minutes.

SERVES 4

PREPARATION + COOKING
30 + 20 minutes

STORAGE
You can keep the baked quiche refrigerated up to 3 days.

TRY THIS WITH...
a side salad as a main meal
in your child's lunchbox.

HIGH IN...
B vitamins, calcium, fiber, magnesium, omega-6 oils, and zinc.

PROPERTIES
Rye flour is a great alternative to the more allergenic wheat flour. It is also extremely effective at stabilizing blood-sugar levels.

moroccan apricot bundles

North African food can be a real hit with kids, as the dried fruit sweetens savory dishes.

SERVES 4

PREPARATION + COOKING
5 + 30 minutes

STORAGE
Refrigerate raw and use within a week, or freeze up to 3 weeks.

TRY THIS WITH...
some fresh green vegetables and couscous for that extra Moroccan feel!

HIGH IN...
B vitamins, beta-carotene, fiber, lycopene, and protein.

PROPERTIES
Apricots are high in both lycopene and beta-carotene, so are doubly protective for the eyes, heart, and skin. Look for healthier unsulfured versions.

1 tablespoon olive oil
½ cup pine nuts
½ red bell pepper, seeded and chopped
2 garlic cloves, thinly sliced
⅔ cup chopped dried apricots
4 scallions, chopped
1 can (14-oz) chickpeas, drained
½ cup crumbled feta cheese
2 tablespoons chopped basil
½ teaspoon freshly ground black pepper
¾ cup crème fraîche or sour cream
10 ounces phyllo dough
1 small egg yolk, beaten

1 Heat the oven to 375°F. Heat the oil in a saucepan. Add the pine nuts, red pepper, and garlic. Sauté 2 minutes, then add the apricots, scallions, and chickpeas. Cook, stirring, over low heat 2 minutes. Remove from the heat.

2 Place the feta in a bowl and mix in the chickpea mixture, basil, black pepper, and crème fraîche.

3 Roll out the phyllo dough large enough to cut four 3- x 3-inch squares. Spoon the mixture into the middle of each square, brush the edges with the egg yolk, fold over to make a triangle, and press the edges together to seal. Bake on a baking sheet 15 to 20 minutes.

pea & parmesan quinoa "risotto"

Quinoa is rich in the amino acids a growing body needs to build proteins. It also provides a healthy dose of cleansing fiber, and serves as a nutritious alternative to rice.

1 cup water
1 teaspoon olive oil
heaped ⅔ cup quinoa
2 tablespoons sesame oil
2 zucchini, sliced
¾ cup chopped asparagus
1 onion, sliced
⅔ cup frozen peas
3 garlic cloves, sliced
heaped 2 teaspoons green peppercorns, rinsed
⅔ cup grated Parmesan cheese

1 Heat the water in a saucepan. Add the olive oil and quinoa and simmer 15 minutes, or until the quinoa becomes thick and all the water is absorbed.

2 Meanwhile, heat the sesame oil in a wok. Add the zucchini, asparagus, and onion and stir-fry over high heat 5 to 6 minutes until the vegetables are soft.

3 Add the peas, garlic, and peppercorns. Reduce the heat and stir-fry 2 minutes longer. Drain the quinoa and add to the wok. Stir in the Parmesan cheese until it melts and serve in individual bowls.

SERVES 4

PREPARATION + COOKING
5 + 15 minutes

STORAGE
This meal is delicious cold and will retain its freshness up to 3 days if refrigerated.

TRY THIS WITH...
a light salad or use as a filler for Pita Pockets (see page 63).

HIGH IN...
B vitamins, fiber, magnesium, potassium, protein.

PROPERTIES
Asparagus is a highly cleansing vegetable and has been used for centuries to support the kidneys. It might be a good idea to explain to your child that it can make their urine smell.

roasted tomato & basil pasta

HIGH IN...
antioxidants, lycopene, and monounsaturated fats.

PROPERTIES
Basil has amazing antibacterial properties, which are found in the aromatic oils that give it its lovely smell. They kill off potentially harmful bacteria.

Tomatoes contain a wealth of vitamin C to increase your child's immune function and the body's ability to heal. A tomato's rich red color comes from another antioxidant substance, lycopene, the therapeutic properties of which actually increase with cooking. Organic tomatoes can contain as much as three times more lycopene to support your child's immune function.

8 ounces fresh spinach tagliatelle (make sure it is egg-free, if necessary)
2 tablespoons olive oil
1 onion, diced
1 garlic clove, thinly sliced
1 can (15-oz) crushed tomatoes
3 ounces cherry tomatoes
1 teaspoon dried oregano
scant 2 cups chopped spinach
2 tablespoons chopped basil
a handful pine nuts

1 Half fill a saucepan with water and bring to a boil. Add the tagliatelle and 1 tablespoon olive oil, cover, and cook until al dente (see package for cooking times).
2 Meanwhile, heat the rest of the olive oil in another pan. Add the onion and garlic and gently sauté.
3 Add the tomatoes, oregano, and spinach and stir over medium heat. Cover and leave to simmer 10 minutes.
4 When the pasta is cooked, drain and arrange on individual plates. Spoon the sauce over the pasta and serve garnished with basil leaves and pine nuts.

SERVES 2

PREPARATION + COOKING
5 + 20 minutes

STORAGE
You can refrigerate the sauce up to 2 days or freeze it up to a month.

TRY THIS WITH...
some spinach for an iron-rich meal.

To slow down sugar-release, try a less-processed, gluten-free pasta, such as buckwheat or corn.

minted potatoes with hazelnuts

SERVES 4

PREPARATION + COOKING
5 + 20 minutes

STORAGE
You can refrigerate up to 3 days.

TRY THIS ...
cold with mayonnaise for potato salad with a twist.

HIGH IN...
B vitamins, fiber, potassium, and vitamin C.

PROPERTIES
Peppermint has amazing calming properties that soothe the gut and help digestion—perfect for any child with an upset tummy.

Adding hazelnuts to potatoes increases the protein and fiber content, slowing down the release of sugars and stabilizing energy levels. Boiled or steamed new potatoes are always a better choice than french fries, but can seem dull to kids. Adding mint and nuts boosts the flavor to appeal to younger tastes.

1 pound 5 ounces new potatoes, scrubbed
⅔ cup whole hazelnuts
2 sprigs mint
2 tablespoons butter
2 tablespoons chopped mint

1 Bring a half-filled saucepan to a boil. Add the potatoes, hazelnuts, and 1 mint sprig, and simmer 15 to 20 minutes until the potatoes are soft. Drain and add the butter and chopped mint, stirring until the butter melts.
2 Pour into a serving dish and garnish with the remaining sprig of mint.

bacon-baked brussels sprouts

Bacon is a popular food with children and adults alike, and while it is very salty, the strong flavor can help to sweeten the pungent taste of Brussels sprouts. The high antioxidant and fiber content of the sprouts will help to offset the fat and salt content of the bacon, while the chestnuts provide an excellent source of plant protein.

14 ounces Brussels sprouts, trimmed and outer leaves removed
8 slices unsmoked bacon, finely chopped
⅔ cup well-drained cooked chestnuts, chopped
⅓ cup chopped prunes
3 tablespoons olive oil

1 Heat the oven to 400°F. Half fill a saucepan with water, bring to a boil. Add the sprouts, cover, and leave to simmer 10 minutes, then drain.

2 Pour the sprouts, bacon, chestnuts, and prunes into a medium baking dish. Drizzle olive oil over the mixture and bake in the oven 20 minutes.

SERVES 4

PREPARATION + COOKING
10 + 30 minutes

STORAGE
You can refrigerate up to 1 day and then reheat.

TRY THIS AS...
a soup by adding vegetable stock and water and processing until smooth in a blender.

HIGH IN...
antioxidants, B vitamins, fiber, protein, and sulfur.

PROPERTIES
Prunes have one of the highest antioxidant properties of all foods, so they are great for protecting against free radicals.

sesame asian greens

SERVES 4

PREPARATION + COOKING
5 + 5 minutes

STORAGE
Refrigerate and use cold in a salad the following day.

TRY THIS WITH...
a portion of noodles for a complete and healthy meal.

HIGH IN...
antioxidants, B vitamins, fiber, omega-6 oils, vitamin E, and zinc.

PROPERTIES
Bean sprouts provide good levels of zinc and B vitamins, because, like your child, they are still growing so all their goodness is concentrated within their small size.

This side dish has a clean taste and crunchy texture, which appeal to kids. Stir-frying helps the meal keep its nutrients, as the vegetable juices form a natural sauce. When you boil vegetables, on the other hand, you usually discard the juices with the cooking water.

3 tablespoons sesame oil
12 ounces bok choy leaves
1 teaspoon chopped gingerroot
8 scallions, chopped
2 cups bean sprouts
2 tablespoons sesame seeds
2 tablespoons tamari soy sauce

1 Heat the oil in a wok. Add the bok choy leaves and stir-fry 2 minutes.

2 Add the ginger, scallions, and bean sprouts and stir continuously over high heat 2 to 3 minutes until the vegetables are tender.

3 Add the sesame seeds and tamari. Remove from the heat and serve in individual bowls.

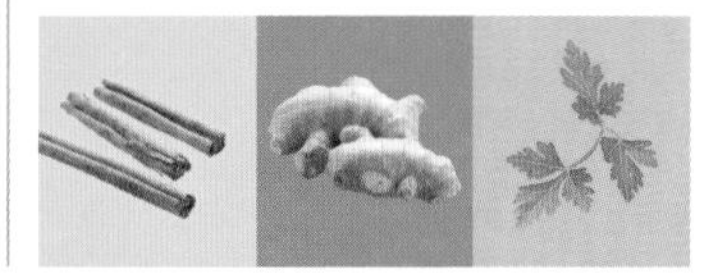

coconut & clove rice

Converting your child from refined, white carbohydrate foods to unrefined versions, such as brown rice, can pose a challenge. With this dish, however, you have help. The sweetness of this side dish, which is great with fish, curries, and lamb, conceals the stronger flavor of brown rice very well.

1½ cups brown basmati rice
½ cup shredded coconut
4 cloves
2 cardamom pods
1 teaspoon cinnamon
2 tablespoons chopped parsley

1 Half fill a saucepan with water and bring to a boil. Add the rice and coconut, cover, and leave to simmer 10 minutes. Drain the rice, rinse with hot water, then return it to the pan.
2 Add the remaining ingredients and 1 tablespoon water. Cover the pan and simmer over low heat 10 minutes, stirring occasionally, until the mixture has the consistency of rice-pudding. Remove from the heat and serve, sprinkled with parsley.

SERVES 4

PREPARATION + COOKING
5 + 20 minutes

STORAGE
Refrigerate this dish overnight, but use within 24 hours.

TRY THIS WITH...
Salmon & Cilantro Fishcakes (see page 47).

HIGH IN...
B vitamins, fiber, magnesium, manganese, selenium, and tryptophan.

PROPERTIES
Brown rice is an excellent source of fiber, B vitamins, and manganese, all crucial for blood-sugar support.

DESSERTS

Desserts, cakes, and other treats are often loaded with refined sugar, saturated fats, and other ingredients that have no—or even negative—nutritional value. In a bid to be "special," party foods in particular are often so laden with additives that they cause hyperactivity and moodiness in children. The great news for parents is that it doesn't have to be this way. The recipes in this chapter contain a few treats, but they are mainly packed with healthy ingredients, such as a variety of different fruits and cinnamon, that provide natural, rather than artificial, sweetness. Nutritious, but nevertheless delicious, they represent the perfect alternatives to additive-rich desserts, cakes, and party foods.

blackberry & apple popsicles

These are a clever way to sneak more fruit into your child's diet. They contain some added sugar, but the nutrients in the fruit help counter the effects. You can use any berry, but blackberries are particularly rich in antioxidants and fiber, which help ease inflammations.

SERVES 4

PREPARATION
20 minutes + freezing

STORAGE
Freeze up to a month.

TRY THIS WITH...
other summer fruits, such as peaches, nectarines, apricots, and strawberries.

HIGH IN...
anthocyanidins, antioxidants, ellagic acid, fiber, and vitamin C.

PROPERTIES
Blackberries contain high levels of ellagic acid, which has been shown to have a strong ability to fight disease and support detoxification.

1 cup water
½ cup packed light brown sugar
2 apples, peeled, cored, and diced
1 cup frozen blackberries
juice of 2 limes

1 Pour the water into a saucepan. Add the sugar and stir until it dissolves.
2 Add the apples, blackberries, and lime juice to the water. Simmer 5 to 7 minutes until the mixture thickens slightly.
3 Remove from the heat and leave to cool for 1 hour. Pour into popsicle molds and freeze.

banana & coconut ice cream

This is a delicious dessert. The sweet coconut reduces the need for additional sugar and the recipe is even dairy-free. Unlike most, this ice cream provides healthy fats and has the added dimension of supporting the immune system.

¼ cup boiling water
2 teaspoons unflavored gelatin
4 tablespoons honey
2 cups vanilla soymilk
2 bananas, mashed
1 teaspoon vanilla extract
½ cup grated fresh coconut
1¾ cups coconut milk

1 Pour the boiling water into a large mixing bowl. Add the gelatin and leave it to dissolve 10 minutes, stirring.

2 Meanwhile, in a saucepan, whisk together the honey and soymilk and stir over low heat 2 minutes until hot. Do not let it boil.

3 Add the gelatin mixture and stir well, then stir in the remaining ingredients. Pour into a bowl and leave to cool 10 minutes before refrigerating at least 3 hours.

4 Spoon the chilled mixture into the canister of an ice-cream maker and process, or pour into a freezerproof container and leave to freeze overnight.

SERVES 4

PREPARATION
15 minutes + cooling + freezing

STORAGE
You can keep ice cream in the freezer up to 2 months.

TRY THIS WITH...
Pumpkin & Orange Crumble (see page 132).

HIGH IN...
beneficial fats, manganese, potassium, and vitamin B6.

PROPERTIES
Coconut contains the mineral manganese, which helps your child's body to produce energy effectively.

orange eskimo bowls

MAKES 10

PREPARATION
30 minutes + freezing

STORAGE
Use within a month from the date of freezing.

TRY THIS WITH...
lemons instead of oranges. or serve with raspberry sauce (see page 126).

HIGH IN...
antioxidants and vitamin C.

PROPERTIES
Citrus fruits contain at least 170 different beneficial plant chemicals and more than 60 antioxidant flavonoids that we know of, making them supremely good for immune function and reducing inflammation.

These little treats are such fun to make—and a real hit at parties. A lot of the goodness in citrus fruit is found in the pith, so scraping away at this to get to the contents adds to the health benefits. The high vitamin-C content of citrus fruits helps to protect against illness and helps with the body's absorption of iron.

10 oranges
grated peel and juice of 1 lemon
grated peel and juice of 1 lime
grated peel and juice of 1 orange
2½ cups boiling water
scant 1 cup packed brown sugar
1 egg white

1 Cut the tops off the oranges and set aside. Scoop out the flesh and juice from 10 of the oranges, discarding this for 8 of them. Place the flesh and the juice of the remaining 2 oranges in a blender and add the juice and grated peel of the lime, lemon, and other orange.
2 In a separate bowl, pour the boiling water onto the sugar and stir to dissolve. Leave to cool before adding to the blender with the egg white, then process until smooth.
3 Pour the mixture into the hollow orange shells, place the tops back on, wrap in plastic wrap, and freeze.

blueberry yogo-pops

The texture and flavor of these popsicles is so close to ice cream children will be forgiven for thinking that they have something much naughtier! Using yogurt that contains live cultures provides even more benefits for your child's digestion and immunity, as it contains higher levels of beneficial bacteria.

2¼ cups plain yogurt with live cultures
scant 1 cup frozen blueberries
juice ½ lime

1 In a bowl mix together the yogurt, blueberries, and lime juice. Pour into popsicle molds and then add the sticks.
2 Place in the freezer a minimum of 2 hours before serving.

SERVES 4

PREPARATION
10 minutes + freezing

STORAGE
Use the yogo-pops within a month of freezing.

TRY THIS WITH...
bananas and strawberries instead of blueberries.

HIGH IN...
anthocyanidins, beneficial bacteria, manganese, and vitamin C.

PROPERTIES
With their deep blue color, blueberries are particularly high in the protective, antioxidant compounds anthocyanidins, which also support the structure of your child's growing tissues and veins.

tropical islands

SERVES 4

PREPARATION
20 minutes + chilling

STORAGE
Refrigerate the gelatin molds up to 4 days. You can refrigerate the raspberry sauce up to a month or, alternatively, freeze it up to a month, if you prefer.

TRY THIS WITH...
other fruit slices, such as peaches, strawberries, oranges or lemons.

HIGH IN...
ellagic acid, iodine, protein, trace minerals, and vitamin C.

PROPERTIES
The iodine in vegetarian gelatin is important for thyroid function, which helps your child produce the energy to grow.

Molded gelatine desserts are making a comeback, and using a vegetarian mix is a much better alternative to conventional gelatin. Made from sea vegetables, vegetarian gelatin is high in protein, the mineral iodine, and other trace minerals. It also sets more quickly than meat-derived gelatin and, most importantly, your child won't know the difference!

1 3-ounce package tropical flavor vegetarian gelatin mix
2½ cups boiling water
1 lime, sliced
¾ cup frozen raspberries
2 tablespoons confectioner's sugar
4 basil leaves

1 Put the gelatin mix in a bowl and pour the boiling water over. Stir the crystals until they dissolve.
2 Place a slice of lime in the bottom of each of 4 ramekins, then fill each with the gelatin. Leave to refrigerate at least 1 hour until the gelatin sets.
3 Blend together the raspberries and confectioner's sugar, then push through a strainer to remove the seeds.
4 Turn out the gelatin molds onto plates and pour raspberry sauce around each. Decorate with a basil leaf.

hawaiian hulas

Cultures that eat more coconut show lower incidence of heart disease and obesity, making this a perfect dessert for today's children.

1¾ cups coconut milk
2 vanilla beans
4 small pineapples
freshly grated meat from ¼ coconut
4 sprigs mint

1 Pour the coconut milk into a bowl, add the vanilla beans and refrigerate 2 hours.

2 Cut off the tops from the pineapples and set aside. Cut out the flesh leaving the skin intact and remove the hard core of the pineapple from the flesh and discard. Chop the flesh into chunks, put 4 chunks to one side and place the rest in a blender. Add the coconut milk and process until smooth. Pour into the pineapple shells.

3 Sprinkle the grated coconut meat into the pineapples. Spear 4 toothpicks with the remaining pineapple and a chunk of coconut. Stick into the side of the pineapple and decorate with mint, then replace the pineapple tops.

SERVES 4

PREPARATION
20 minutes + chilling

STORAGE
Keep for no longer than 24 hours in the refrigerator.

TRY THIS WITH...
slices of mango and banana.

HIGH IN...
beneficial fats (triglycerides, which the body uses as energy), manganese, potassium, and vitamin B6.

PROPERTIES
High in potassium, coconut is a natural isotonic: it has a similar mineral content to our own blood plasma, so it helps to keep mineral levels at their optimum. It is also rehydrating.

watermelon zest

SERVES 4

PREPARATION
10 minutes

STORAGE
You can refrigerate up to 24 hours.

TRY THIS WITH...
some sliced banana and pineapple for a really fruity dish.

HIGH IN...
beta-carotene, lycopene, potassium, and vitamins A, B1, B6, and C.

PROPERTIES
Watermelon is rich in vitamins A and C and very low in calories—great for all the family.

This is a really refreshing and vibrant dessert that is easy to make for parties. The intense red color of watermelon comes from its high level of lycopene, the same antioxidant substance that gives tomatoes their redness.

1 watermelon
3 passion fruit
3 limes

1 Cut the watermelon lengthwise, then cut into triangular slices or cubes, removing the skin. Place the watermelon pieces onto a large plate.
2 Cut the passion fruit in half. Scoop out the flesh with a spoon into a small bowl and remove the seeds. Squeeze the juice from two of the limes and add to the passion fruit. Mix together, then pour the mixture evenly over the melon.
3 Cut the remaining lime in half, then into wedges and decorate the edge of the plate with these.

V

tropical fruit kabobs

Like the bromelain in pineapple, papaya contains a protein-digesting enzyme called papain. Papaya and pineapple are therefore particularly good to eat after a meal rich in dense proteins, such as red meats, especially if your child suffers from gas or bloating.

4 ounces raspberries
2 tablespoons light brown sugar
⅓ cup water
1 pineapple
2 papaya
4 kiwi fruit
4 limes

1 Put the raspberries, sugar, and water in a saucepan and bring to a boil, then leave to simmer 10 to 15 minutes until the mixture thickens. Remove from the heat, press through a strainer, and put in the refrigerator to cool 2 hours.
2 Cut the skin and top off the pineapple and papaya. Remove the seeds from the papaya and discard. Chop the fruit into 1-inch cubes. Peel the kiwi fruit and cut into thick slices. Cut the limes in half, and then into slices.
3 Spear the fruit onto 8 skewers, alternating pineapple, kiwi, papaya, and lime until the skewers are full.
4 Place two kabobs on each plate. Decorate with a slice of lime and drizzle the raspberry sauce over the kabobs.

SERVES 4

PREPARATION + COOKING
10 + 15 minutes

STORAGE
Keep refrigerated up to 12 hours.

TRY THIS WITH...
other fruits, such as strawberries, banana, melon, and apple.

HIGH IN...
antioxidants, fiber, manganese, protein-digesting enzymes, and vitamin C.

PROPERTIES
Bromelain, papain, and vitamin C all have anti-inflammatory properties that help relieve symptoms of eczema, asthma, and psoriasis.

berry juicy yogurt

HIGH IN...
anthocyanidins, beneficial bacteria, fiber, manganese, and vitamin C.

PROPERTIES
All berries have high levels of vitamin C and antioxidants, which help to prevent diseases, such as cancer, later in life.

A mixture of berries is a welcome addition to any child's diet. The deep, rich colors provide plenty of protective anthocyanidins to encourage good memory and learning and also to improve circulation and heart health. In addition, berries have been shown to be extremely brain-protective and they also support liver function, to help banish toxins from your child's body.

SERVES 4

PREPARATION
10 minutes

STORAGE
You can refrigerate up to 24 hours.

TRY THIS WITH...
chopped strawberries or blackberries.

1¾ cups plain yogurt with live cultures
juice of 1 lime
½ cup granola, or similar "oat crunchy" cereal
2 cups summer fruits, such as blueberries, strawberries, and raspberries
4 sprigs mint

1 Pour the yogurt into a large mixing bowl. Stir in the lime juice. Add the granola and mix thoroughly with a wooden spoon.

2 Spoon 2 tablespoons of the yogurt into each of 4 glasses, then spoon in 2 tablespoons of the summer fruits. Repeat these layers until each glass is full, finishing with a layer of yogurt with a small dollop of summer fruits on top.

3 Decorate each glass with a sprig of mint.

A child who is gluten intolerant might also react to the granola. Try a gluten-free version.

pumpkin & orange crumble

Nutrient-packed pumpkin is a real superfood, and works just as well in a sweet dish as a savory one. This might not be your usual dessert fare, but give it a try at least once!

SERVES 4

PREPARATION + COOKING
15 + 40 minutes

STORAGE
Freeze the unbaked dish up to a month.

TRY THIS WITH...
sour cream or Banana and Coconut Ice Cream (see page 123).

HIGH IN...
beta-carotene, calcium, iron, magnesium, manganese, vitamins A and C, and zinc.

PROPERTIES
The manganese in pumpkin provides antioxidants to help protect against free radicals, while the iron improves oxygenation in the blood.

1 cup self-rising flour
¾ cup packed light brown sugar
½ stick butter, diced
2 eggs
1 teaspoon cinnamon
¼ teaspoon ground ginger
1¼ cups evaporated milk
2½ cups peeled and chopped pumpkin
3 oranges, peeled and flesh roughly chopped

1 Heat the oven to 350°F. Place the flour and ¼ cup of the sugar in a bowl. Add the butter and use your fingers to mix together until the mixture becomes like bread crumbs.
2 In a mixing bowl, beat the eggs with a fork and add the spices, evaporated milk, and remaining sugar.
3 Put the pumpkin and oranges into a baking dish with a high rim. Pour the milk and spice mix on top, then cover with the crumblike topping. Place the dish in the oven and bake 30 to 40 minutes until the top becomes golden brown. Remove from the oven and serve hot.

spiced apple volcanoes

Believe it or not, apples are a good source of protein, which insures a steady release of the sugars in the apples into your child's body.

4 cooking apples, cored
¾ cup golden raisins
4 tablespoons pine nuts
12 cloves
2 teaspoons ground cinnamon
4 tablespoons maple syrup
2½ cups milk
2 vanilla beans
6 egg yolks
¼ cup packed light brown sugar

1 Heat the oven to 425°F. Line a baking sheet with foil, keeping enough spare foil around the sides to cover the apples. Place the apples on the sheet. For each apple, pierce the skin with 3 cloves. Fill with raisins and pine nuts. Sprinkle the cinnamon over and drizzle with maple syrup. Wrap in the foil and bake 15 minutes.
2 Meanwhile, heat the milk in a saucepan but do not boil. Add the vanilla beans and leave to infuse 10 minutes.
3 Break the egg yolks into a bowl. Add the sugar and whisk until thick. Remove the vanilla beans from the milk. Slowly beat the milk into the egg. Pour into a nonstick pan and cook over low heat, stirring, until thick. Remove the apples from the oven and serve with the custard sauce.

SERVES 4

PREPARATION + COOKING
10 + 15 minutes

STORAGE
Eat immediately. Once cored, you can keep the apples overnight in a bowl of cold water with a squeeze of lemon to prevent them from browning.

TRY THIS WITH...
an organic, dairy-free ice cream.

HIGH IN...
B vitamins, fiber, selenium, tryptophan, and vitamins C and K.

PROPERTIES
The soluble and insoluble forms of fiber in apples make them perfect for regulating bowel movements.

bread, butter & honey pudding

SERVES 4

PREPARATION + COOKING
10 + 30 minutes

STORAGE
You can freeze this before cooking and keep it up to a month. After cooking keep it up to 3 days in the refrigerator.

TRY THIS WITH...
a dollop of plain or Greek yogurt or custard sauce.

HIGH IN...
B vitamins, calcium, fiber, magnesium, omega-3 and -6 oils, and zinc.

PROPERTIES
Pumpkin seeds provide high levels of zinc, which in the ground help the pumpkin to grow. It will do the same for your child.

This healthy twist on an old favorite uses wholegrain bread for more fiber. This recipe is ideal for kids who won't normally eat such bread—it's disguised visually and through its sweet flavor.

14 ounces wholewheat bread
½ stick butter
scant ½ cup clear honey
3 tablespoons raisins
2 tablespoons pine nuts
2 tablespoons pumpkin seeds
1¼ cups soymilk
3 eggs
1 teaspoon cinnamon

1 Heat the oven to 425°F. Cut the bread into 11 slices, then spread with butter and honey, and remove the crusts. Cut each slice into two triangles.
2 In a bowl, combine the raisins, pine nuts, and pumpkin seeds. Line the bottom of a baking dish with the bread slices. Sprinkle a handful of the nut/raisin mixture over. Continue to alternate layers until the dish is full.
3 In another bowl, whisk together the soymilk, eggs and cinnamon. Pour over the bread and leave to stand 10 minutes. Bake 20 to 30 minutes until golden brown. Serve immediately.

toffee apple crisps

Using oats as the basis for a treat really helps keep the sugar rush of sweet foods in check. Oats are a very low glycemic food, which means they release their sugars slowly, holding back the blood-sugar surge that is the usual result of eating sweet foods. Using molasses to sweeten also provides minerals to aid blood-sugar regulation.

½ stick butter
2 tablespoons blackstrap molasses
2 tablespoons light corn syrup
1¼ cups rolled oats
2 apples, grated

1 Heat the oven to 325°F. Place the butter, molasses, and syrup in a small saucepan and melt over low heat. Put the oats and grated apple in a mixing bowl, add the melted mixture, and stir.

2 Put teaspoon-size balls of the mixture onto a greased baking sheet and bake 15 minutes, or until golden brown. Leave to cool on wire racks.

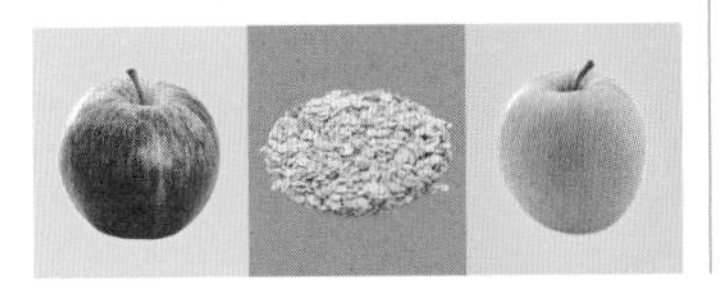

MAKES 10

PREPARATION + COOKING
10 + 15 minutes

STORAGE
Can be stored in an airtight container up to 2 weeks.

TRY THIS WITH...
some sour cream
or plain yogurt.

HIGH IN...
calcium, fiber, iron, manganese, potassium, selenium, and tryptophan.

PROPERTIES
Oats contain a fiber called beta-glucans, which significantly helps to remove toxins from your child's body.

V

gingerbread star cookies

MAKES 12 TO 15

PREPARATION + COOKING
15 + 20 minutes

STORAGE
Store in an airtight container up to 2 weeks.

TRY THIS...
crumbled as a topping over ice cream.

HIGH IN...
antioxidants.

PROPERTIES
Ginger is a potent anti-inflammatory agent and it also increases circulation.

The allspice and ginger in these cookies help to reduce the harmful effects of the sugar with their anti-inflammatory and antioxidant actions. The cookies are rich and satisfying, so children won't want to eat too many.

3 tablespoons butter
¼ cup packed brown sugar
⅓ cup light corn syrup
1 cup all-purpose flour
1 teaspoon ground ginger
½ teaspoon allspice
½ teaspoon baking powder

1 Heat the oven to 350°F. Place the butter, sugar, and syrup in a small saucepan and melt over low heat. Place the remaining ingredients in a bowl and pour in the melted mixture.

2 Mix with a wooden spoon until the dough leaves the side of the bowl. Roll out on a lightly floured countertop and cut out 12 to 15 cookies with a star-shaped cutter. Place the cookies on a nonstick cookies sheet and bake 15 to 20 minutes until golden. Remove from the oven and leave to cool on wire racks.

V

jammy heart tarts

Even small changes can make a difference, like choosing pure fruit strawberry jam for these tarts. Commercial jams tend to be made with a "strawberry-flavored" sugary gloop, which might not contain any real fruit at all. Check labels for the highest amount of fruit per 100g of jam, or use a fruit puree.

1 cup all-purpose flour
¼ cup packed light brown sugar
½ stick butter, diced
2 tablespoons water
½ cup pure fruit strawberry jam

1 Heat the oven to 400°F. Place the flour, sugar and butter in a large bowl and mix together using your fingertips.
2 Add 1 tablespoon of water and mix well. If the mixture is not holding together, add the other tablespoon of water. Press the dough together and knead for a few minutes until it holds. Carefully roll out the dough on a lightly floured countertop.
3 Cut out 12 to 15 circles using a medium round cutter. Grease the same number of nonstick heart-shaped tartlette pans. Press the circles of dough into the pans and put 1 heaped teaspoon jam into each tart. Bake 15 to 20 minutes until the pastry is golden. Remove from the oven and cool on wire racks.

MAKES 12 TO 15 TARTS

PREPARATION + COOKING
15 + 20 minutes

STORAGE
Store the tarts in an airtight container up to 2 weeks.

TRY THIS WITH...
apricot jam or an extra half strawberry on top to serve.

HIGH IN...
ellagic acid, manganese, and vitamins C and K.

PROPERTIES
Strawberries are high in ellagic acid and antioxidants, both of which will boost your child's immune system and protect the liver.

V

fruity chocolate fondue

This dessert looks amazing, tastes delicious, and has a high fruit content. In short, it is the ideal healthy party food.

SERVES 8

PREPARATION
25 minutes

STORAGE
You can refrigerate the dips up to 2 days, but eat the fruit immediately.

TRY THIS WITH...
any fruit, and experiment with the dips by adding crushed nuts, as long as your child is more than 5 years old.

HIGH IN...
beta-carotene, fiber, manganese, potassium, and vitamin C.

PROPERTIES
Bananas are a great source of vitamin B6, which is necessary for energy production and helps to make the feel-good hormone serotonin.

10 ounces strawberries
6 bananas
2 pineapples
8 peaches
¾ cup plus 2 tablespoons coconut milk
¾ cup plus 2 tablespoons cream cheese
½ teaspoon vanilla extract
¼ cup packed light brown sugar
6 ounces good-quality milk chocolate
1 teaspoon unsweetened cocoa powder
2 sprigs mint

1 Peel all the fruit, except the strawberries and peaches, and cut into 1-inch chunks.

2 Put the coconut milk, vanilla extract, sugar, and half the cream cheese into a blender and process until smooth.

3 Melt the chocolate in a saucepan over very low heat. Stir in the remaining cream cheese and cocoa powder.

4 Pour the two dips into separate bowls and place them in the middle of a large serving platter. Arrange the fruit around the bowls, alternating colors. Decorate the dips with sprigs of mint and serve with toothpicks.

party cake

Adding nuts and cinnamon helps to reduce the amount of sugar you need in baking, and regulates blood sugar—making this cake ideal for a moodiness-free celebration.

1⅔ cups self-rising flour
1 teaspoon ground cinnamon
1 teaspoon ground nutmeg
1 stick butter
⅓ cup chopped walnuts
⅓ cup raisins
2 apples, cored and grated
1 tablespoon grated lemon peel
3 eggs
¼ cup apple juice

1 Heat the oven to 350°F and grease a 9- x 5-in loaf pan. In a bowl combine the flour, cinnamon, nutmeg, and butter and mix well, rubbing between fingers.

2 Stir in the walnuts, raisins, and apple. Add the grated lemon peel, eggs, and juice. Beat with a wooden spoon until combined. Pour the batter into the loaf pan and smooth the surface. Place in the oven and bake 40 to 50 minutes, or until the cake is well risen and light brown. Leave to cool on a wire rack.

SERVES 10

PREPARATION + COOKING
15 + 50 minutes

STORAGE
You can store the cake in a refrigerator up to 3 weeks.

TRY THIS WITH...
the citrus frosting in the Bunny Bites recipe (see page 140).

HIGH IN...
B vitamins, calcium, magnesium, omega-3 and -6 oils, and zinc.

PROPERTIES
Walnuts are among the best plant sources of omega-3 oils and have been shown to boost mental function and to be a potent natural antidepressant.

bunny bites

HIGH IN...
antioxidants, B vitamins, beta-carotene, boron, calcium, fiber, magnesium, and omega-3 and -6 oils.

PROPERTIES
Golden raisins are a good way to sweeten baked goods, and they provide good levels of the mineral boron, essential for bone growth.

The cinnamon, carrot, walnuts, eggs, and ginger in this recipe help to slow down the release of the sugars into the bloodstream. These ingredients also provide therapeutic benefits for your child's digestion, immune system, and brain development.

MAKES 12

PREPARATION + COOKING
10 + 30 minutes

STORAGE
Keep the cupcakes without frosting up to 4 days in an airtight container. Once frosted, it is best to eat them within 3 days.

TRY THIS WITH...
a half-apple and half-carrot batter instead of all carrot, or add mashed bananas.

½ cup olive oil
½ cup packed dark brown sugar
1 teaspoon cinnamon
½ teaspoon ginger
½ cup crushed walnuts
⅓ cup golden raisins
1⅓ cups peeled and grated carrot
grated peel of 2 oranges
1 cup plus 2 tablespoons self-rising flour
2 eggs
1 teaspoon vanilla extract
2 tablespoons butter
½ cup cream cheese
scant ¾ cup confectioner's sugar
grated peel of 1 lemon
½ tablespoon lemon juice

1 Heat the oven to 400°F. Put the oil, sugar, spices, walnuts, golden raisins, carrot, and half the orange peel into a bowl. Stir and then add the flour, eggs, and vanilla extract and beat until smooth.

2 Line a 12-cup cupcake pan with paper liners and divide the batter evenly. Bake in the oven 30 minutes, or until light golden. Leave to cool 30 minutes on wire racks.

3 Meanwhile, make the frosting. Put the remaining ingredients, reserving some of the lemon peel, into a bowl and cream together. Spread 1 tablespoon of frosting on each bunny bite, then decorate with the remaining peel.

Many health-food stores sell egg substitutes specifically designed for cake baking.

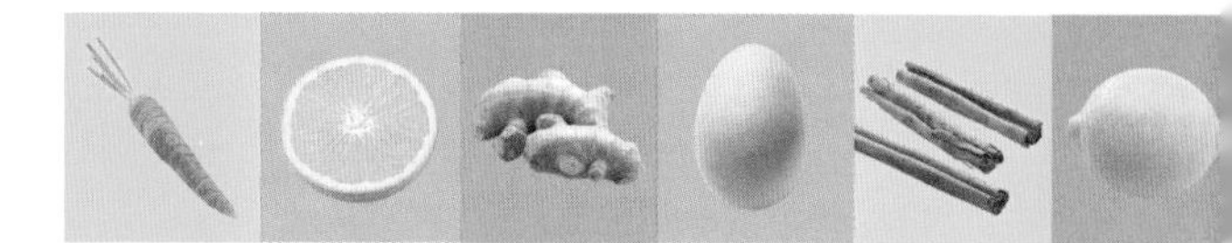

index

AUTHORS' ACKNOWLEDGMENTS

Charlotte Watts
So many thanks to Mark and Dad for their support, interest, and ongoing patience!

Gemini Adams
With deep gratitude to Granny Hambly and Granny Glasses, who spared so much time and knowledge sharing their culinary wisdom and wizardry with me.